SHRUB ROSES
Paradise in Bloom

SHRUB ROSES

Paradise in Bloom

MARILYN RAFF

JOHNSON BOOKS • *Boulder*

Published by Johnson Books, a division of Big Earth Publishing
    3005 Center Green Drive, Suite 220
    Boulder, Colorado 80301
    E-mail: books@bigearthpublishing.com
    www.johnsonbooks.com

Cover and text design by Polly Christensen

9   8   7   6   5   4   3   2   1

Library of Congress Cataloging-in-Publication Data
Raff, Marilyn.
    Shrub roses : paradise in bloom / Marilyn Raff.
p. cm.
Includes bibliographical references and index.
    ISBN 1-55566-381-8
    1. Shrub roses. 2. Rose culture. I. Title.
SB411.65.S45R34 2006
635.9'33734—dc22   2006005668

Printed in Malaysia

With love —
Gabe, Rachel, Gloria, and Andy

Acknowledgments

I AM GRATEFUL TO VARIOUS PEOPLE for assisting me by sharing their expertise about shrub roses. The topic is quite complex and sometimes had me spinning as I tried to untangle roses from the past and present. The late Bill Campbell, rosarian extraordinaire, was especially helpful, as were Heather Campbell, Harriett McMillan, Peggy Williams, Marilyn Wells, Merle Moore, Eve and Mikl Brawner, Kay Galvan, Al Ford, and Tom Carter. Rosarian Marlea Graham was excellent with details and technical information related to roses. I thank Leslie Heizer for her encouragement and assistance with the manuscript. Marlene Blessing was indeed that, a blessing. An excellent editor, she helped me fine-tune portions of my manuscript. I've enjoyed the fun and challenge of writing this book. Learning the historical background of roses has been a fascinating, in-depth process!

Contents

A friend took this photograph—
it is a sign at a flower shop in
Santa Fe, New Mexico.

INTRODUCTION

The Spellbinding Heritage of Roses

ANYONE CAN GROW ROSES. Yes, it's true! Some people believe that roses are a burden for the gardener, because of their false reputation for being high-maintenance plants that need to be sprayed, are hard to prune, get various diseases, and eventually succumb to the cold of winter—especially if snow cover is sparse, your winter watering schedule is less than ideal, and they have not been sufficiently mulched! All of this sounds discouraging. And it is largely true if you grow only the fussier hybrid teas and floribundas. But there are many more roses from which to choose. With some basic knowledge, you can find the best low-maintenance rose to match your garden situation, lifestyle, climate, as well as your heart's desire. I will introduce you to roses that will work for you whether you garden round the clock or merely dabble in the dirt on the weekends.

In this book, I cover the basics of growing roses clearly and simply, sprinkling in historical facts and myths and keeping technical information to a minimum. Through teaching classes on roses, I have discovered that most rose fanciers have two concerns: is the rose fragrant, and do the blooms repeat continuously from summer into fall? I will focus on three main areas: 1) hardy, easy-care roses for cold climates; 2) how to combine roses creatively with a wide range of other plant material; and 3) rose successes and failures that most gardeners can relate to that offer experiential wisdom. For gardeners new to roses, I also devote a chapter to planting techniques, soil amendment, pruning, and other basic maintenance tasks.

I didn't come from a gardening background. In truth, I didn't know an annual from a perennial when I began to garden. But in my late thirties, I became curious about flowers. One sunny day, I wandered casually into the Denver Botanic Gardens, where rock gardens captured my interest. For many years thereafter, I volunteered, working with experts in the field, slowly learning the ins and outs of rock gardening, as well as other phases of hands-on garden work, such as soil amendment and how to care for and grow perennials and bulbs. For more than a decade, I was consumed with small plants and their unique shapes, textures, and colors.

Then I was ready for something different—and bigger. The Denver Botanic Gardens' education department offered classes on roses. I took a few of these and, with some knowledge under my belt, began to grow roses in my garden. I remember experimenting with 'Helen Traubel', an apricot and pink gem, in addition to another variety whose name has faded into oblivion. These roses lasted for a few seasons, but often needed frequent coddling or died over the winter. In one class I attended, I distinctly recall that the instructor was covered head to toe in what looked like riot gear! I learned these coveralls, plus a mask, were to protect gardeners from getting chemicals on their skin and inhaling dangerous fumes. The instructor spent an hour discussing methods to care for these fussy roses, explaining techniques to battle pests and diseases such as thrips, spider mites, leaf rollers, botrytis, and many other unpronounceable ills. That class turned me off permanently to hybrid teas; but I still wanted to grow roses. I began researching roses that would do well in the roller-coaster climate of the Intermountain West. Once I found a winning hand with old garden roses (those introduced prior to 1867 and sometimes known as old-fashioned, heritage, or antique roses), species (or wild roses) and modern roses (those bred after 1867), my passion for roses ignited. Although hybrid teas and floribundas are included under modern roses, I avoided these two groups because they require too much maintenance.

As my interest in roses developed, I began thumbing through mail-order catalogs. With gusto I read descriptions and gushed over colorful rose pictures. Soon, I was ordering roses from the East and West Coasts, in addition to exploring local sources. I usually ordered plants in January, sitting in my cozy house while winter crawled too

The flashy pink petals of 'Nearly Wild' rose are even more attractive when mixed among the darkened and flamboyant blossoms of pinks (*Dianthus barbatus* 'Nigricans').

Rose 'Applejack' is surrounded by the deep pink flowers of *Geranium* 'Patricia'.

An unknown red rose and blue oat grass (*Helictotrichon sempervirens*) are the cornerstones of this captivating vignette.

The delicate, curved petals of *Rosa spinosissima* play off well against the finely textured leaves.

Rose 'Maiden's Blush' sparkles in the sunlight and is especially attractive next to the darkened flowers of pinks (*Dianthus barbatus* 'Nigricans').

The peachy-pink, lavender-tinged flowers of 'Nymphenburg' rose are complemented by the voluptuous blooms of poppy (*Papaver orientale* 'Royal Wedding').

A mass planting of 'Sea Foam' rose is attractive next to flagstone.

'Complicata' rose is picture-perfect next to the buttery yellow blossoms of *Rosa foetida persiana*.

The tall form of coreopsis winds among the robust blossoms of 'Désirée Parmentier' rose, while the yellow blooms of *Rosa foetida persiana* remain in the background.

slowly through the landscape. Finally, in late April, my roses arrived clothed in slightly moist newspaper. I was all smiles as I carefully unwrapped the damp newspaper from the eight-inch stems and tiny leaves that soon would mature in my garden among other roses, perennials, and rock garden plants.

My love of old garden roses and other shrub roses—a catchall term used by many rose enthusiasts to encompass a wide range of types—solidified when, in 1994, I went to England on a rose tour. I met my rose mentor, the late Graham Stuart Thomas, who I remember fondly, and chatted with him briefly. As I traveled with a group of twenty rose-hungry travelers, plus an expert rosarian to guide us, I was wide-eyed with wonder when I encountered the great rose gardens of England. These included the historic Castle Howard, built in 1699, with ten thousand acres of land where vistas were lined with hundreds of shrub roses. In the mid-1970s, Mottisfont Abbey became another haven for roses. It is an ancient

manor house, which has been chiefly known for its large collection of old garden roses, species roses, and many modern roses. Most of England receives at least thirty inches of moisture annually, so the roses were quite different in terms of size and shape than those I saw in the dry or semiarid landscapes of Colorado. Nevertheless, their rich colors and lavish displays helped thrust me more deeply into the world of roses, and I have been enamored of them ever since.

The hundred-plus roses that I grow in my Littleton garden in the Rocky Mountain West will adapt to various gardens and climates across the country, mostly in regions that have some period of chilling; i.e., a time when temperatures go below freezing or hover near 32 degrees. Many of my roses have survived temperatures down to minus 25 degrees. I'm sure that even if temperatures became colder, these roses would survive because they are shrubs on their own roots (please see discussion further on about "own-root" roses). However,

When planted in separate sections of the landscape, especially with a path in between, rock gardens and perennial borders have a compatible relationship.

In a woodland setting, red valerian (*Centranthus ruber*) and unknown shrub roses bloom abundantly and create a sensational scene.

extra care helps their survival, such as more mulch and extra watering. These factors and others, such as sun and soil conditions, influence the survival of roses. Sometimes, even if a shrub rose dies all the way to the ground, the rose will rejuvenate because it is an own-root rose.

Important, too, is location. A particular microclimate in your garden can be critical to a rose's survival. Plant a rose in a protected or warmer spot, near a large tree or on the southern side of a garage or a house. Sites such as these have microclimates, which are small or large climatic niches with very particular conditions of sunlight, moisture, heat, and soil. By taking advantage of planting in the most ideal microclimates in your garden, a rose that might ordinarily die at 10 degrees

below zero will ignore the overall climatic conditions in the garden and thrive in the warmer microclimate in which you've planted it. This is one of the gardener's best tricks to coax roses to grow in cold regions. Or perhaps your garden is exposed to extensive wind, or maybe bountiful amounts of snow settle in particular areas and too much water accumulates in these spots in spring and summer. You may not want to plant in those particular sites. Again, search out more favorable pockets of ground around your existing property that enjoy microclimates where your rose will receive greater protection from the elements. How much TLC (tender loving care) or effort do you want to give to your rose? This is a question that each gardener must decide.

The green leaves and red blooms of 'Niobe' clematis twine among the white flowers of 'Darlow's Enigma' rose.

Near the fence, the flowers of 'Nevada' rose bloom. A red peony presents a stark contrast to the rose, as shrubby *Clematis recta*, with its star-shaped blossoms, sits off to the left.

For gardeners in warmer sections or southern parts of the country, where temperatures may not dip near freezing and moisture levels are significantly higher than those in the Rocky Mountain region, I know there are shrub roses that adapt specifically to your region, and many from my book will work for you. However, you might have to be a bit of a "Sherlock Holmes" to discover which ones are best. As far as care of your roses goes, if your area receives 40 to 60 inches of moisture and winters are mild, common sense will help you understand that you should not do extra watering or add mulch, which would contribute to diseases and pests. There are unique growing conditions in each part of the country. For each region there are particular garden practices to help you and your roses cope with variable climatic conditions.

I recommend rose lovers check with their local extension services. Each state and specific counties have horticultural offices staffed by people who have studied agriculture and horticulture in depth, and know the particulars of what succeeds in your backyard. They will tell you which roses, along with other plants, grow best in your region. Moreover, I encourage gardeners to join garden clubs and talk with fellow gardeners and rose growers: learn exactly which roses have adapted for them and what levels of care were required for each. Another excellent source of garden wisdom is your local library and, where possible, a botanic garden. Finally, rose-growing companies are top-notch resources (see the catalog listings at the end of this book). Contact them directly for rose recommendations: describe for them your area's temperature ranges and other variable conditions, and they will inform you which roses will thrive in your region.

Historical Roots

I think of old garden roses as antiques that grow. Their roots grip the earth, spread in all directions, then shoot up canes with abandon, becoming ground covers, climbers, and shrubs of many distinctive shapes, sizes, and colors. To enjoy these living antiques, all you have to do is learn a few simple techniques (see Chapter Six), dig a hole, and plant them in your garden. Easy. Unlike inorganic and more familiar antiques, such as furniture and cars, where investment can be costly, these roses are relatively inexpensive. Their value is that they mature and thrive for decades and may often, with minimal care, outlive the gardener who planted them! This is evident in neglected gardens and old homesteads where plant material, such as roses and irises, keeps chugging along. Oblivious to intense heat, snow, wind, and other weather-related conditions, the plants continue to produce rainbows of beautiful blooms.

Old garden roses and species roses have been around for centuries, passed from generation to generation via cuttings and seeds from rose enthusiasts. Some rosarians feel these two classes of roses have worn out their welcome. Many of these roses bloom for only a few weeks, usually in June, and thereafter, until the following year, their lush foliage acts as a backdrop to any garden scheme. Other rose lovers believe that, despite this so-called imperfection, these "once-

The soft blossoms of 'Martin Frobisher' rose contrast with the single petals of Armenian poppy (*Papaver triniifolium*).

bloomers" will always have a place in our hearts and in our gardens, because many have well-endowed blooms, plush perfume, and a fascinating historical background. These classics may be less popular today because the recent rose market has been saturated with new shrub roses that are ever-blooming, fragrant, disease-resistant, and grower-friendly. In any case, the glorious close-up photographs in garden and rose catalogs and on Web sites, extract the essence of each enticing blossom, luring gardeners into purchasing these newcomers.

The classification distinctions among old garden, species, and modern roses can be quite complex and a bit blurry at times. One expert rosarian slots a rose in one category, while another expert may determine it belongs elsewhere. Some experts will agree with my categorizations of certain roses, while others will take issue with them. But for most rose lovers, the beauty, scents, and blossoms draw us to these awesome plants, not their classifications. In *Shrub Roses: Paradise in Bloom*, we will take a tour of my garden. I have grouped the roses according to my research. We will discover the essential characteristics of each rose and learn how it looks and performs for me as well as in the gardens of colleagues and friends.

All roses have their origins in prehistoric times. Rose fossils have been found in North America, Europe, and Asia—some dating back 35 million years. Just a few hours' drive from where I have lived for twenty-five years is the town of Florissant, Colorado. Here, stored in a museum under lock and key, are famous rose fossils that display in detail the leaf and stem forms of ancient specimens. I feel honored to be growing living pieces of history in my suburban neighborhood, only a short distance from where prehistoric specimens were uncovered.

Roses connect us to bygone times as well as to ancient historical figures, places, and events. When I grow old garden roses, I feel connected to various people from the past. For instance, Theophrastus (ca. 372–ca. 287 B.C.), philosopher, scientist, and first major botanical writer, described roses in detail, discussing propagating techniques as well as blossoming periods in Egypt. He records that in some gardens, known as "Gardens of Adonis," exceptionally pretty roses were cultivated in silver pots. I, too, like to showcase noteworthy roses, such as 'Golden Wings', with its saucer-shaped, lemon-yellow blooms accentuated by spidery golden stamens. This rose stands out in one of my raised berms, towering a few feet above various perennials and ground covers. In earlier civilizations, roses were not only admired for their beauty and scent, but also were valued for their medicinal and cosmetic uses, as well as in cooking, where rose petals were transformed slowly into luscious delicacies such as rose syrup and jam. In addition, gravesites were adorned by roses, a tradition that has continued into the present.

I like believing that the elegant ancient rose that dominates my front garden, *Rosa* x *alba* 'Semiplena', is perhaps one of the roses that the Greek physician Dioscorides, living in the first century A.D., referred to when he wrote an herbal text about the medicinal uses of plants and included several references to rose petals and rose hips. I imagine that the large flasklike red hips of 'Semiplena' might have been used for curing sore throats and headaches, among other ailments. Dioscorides also mentions that the vigorous, once-blooming *Rosa canina* was named so because it was thought to cure rabies. Knowing I am a rose lover, a local nurseryman recently passed this rose on to me when it was about to be bulldozed under to make way for another housing development. I have secured it atop a strong trellis, letting it wind its way through a fence, as it stretches its long canes upward, framing one corner of my backyard.

In ancient Roman times, revelers wore rose wreaths on their heads and used roses in garlands; roses also decorated arenas where spectators sat in boxes at large public gatherings. Legend has it that during a feast, Roman Emperor Elagabalus had an excessive amount of rose petals poured on his guests, who were suffocated by their weight and volume! While dining, Romans reclined on ornate cushions filled with rose petals and nourished themselves with such culinary delights as rose-flavored jellies, puddings, wine, and water. Dried rose petals have also been used for years in potpourri. I recall the ancient Romans when I tuck potpourri sachets in drawers and closets. In my house, I have a few finely cut glass bowls strategically placed in different rooms, filled with colorful dried rose petals. In the dead of winter, when the garden is chilled and draped in snow and icicles, it's a pleasure to inhale the scent of roses.

Based on finds at excavation sites in Rome, roses were imprinted on more than one hundred different Roman coins over several centuries. The Romans were excellent gardeners, who learned to force roses into bloom in the winter by growing them in greenhouses or by watering them with warm water.

An unknown Alba rose, with pinkish and white floppy blossoms is dressy among deep green leaves.

I also feel a connection with Empress Josephine, wife of Napoleon, who in the 1800s was famous for her impressive collection of species and old garden roses. She was instrumental in fostering the popularity of these roses, and her private collection numbered more than two hundred fifty varieties of roses. At her elaborate mansion near Paris—Malmaison—she attempted to grow every variety known in her day. Napoleon made contributions on occasion by sending back plants and seeds from his military expeditions. While each of my rose purchases represents something of an adventure, I'm grateful that my rose gathering forays are less hazardous than those of Napoleon.

Legends about roses abound. Although I have read the following story in more than one source, I remain skeptical, strongly believing it to be myth. The story goes like this: Christopher Columbus was on the verge of discovering the New World. He was weary from his long travels. As he stood on the deck of his ship in the turbulent Sargasso

In autumn, the crimson leaves and burgundy stems of 'Metis' rose combine pleasingly with the light pink blossoms of 'Clara Curtis' chrysanthemum.

Sea northeast of the West Indies, he happened to see a rose branch floating in the water. This sighting gave him the courage to continue searching for the New World. He rightly believed that land was not far off since he found this woody plant material intact enough to discern that it was from a rose bush.

Whether fact or fiction, these stories are fascinating. From their prehistoric beginnings, to centuries past when ancient civilizations were captured by their beauty, scent, and usefulness, to the today's wealth of rose offerings, roses continue to attract gardeners throughout the world.

CHAPTER ONE

Species Roses and Their Hybrids: Mother Nature's Naturals

SPECIES ROSES are the living ancestors of all roses. Gardeners, hikers, and other lovers of the outdoors see species roses (more commonly known as wild roses) growing in the mountains, on the plains, and throughout many parts of the world. Except for one species that has four petals, these rose flowers are composed of five petals.

Technically speaking, roses that have five to eleven petals are considered single; roses with twelve to twenty-three petals are semidouble; double roses have twenty-four to fifty petals. Very double roses have more than fifty petals. The shapes of the blossoms can be further classified as cupped, expanded, globular, and reflexed. One subdivision that I favor is called "quartered." These blossoms look neatly and somewhat evenly divided into four quarters, like a pie might be. For simplicity's sake, I will mostly restrict my descriptions to single, semidouble, and double. Occasionally, I will mention those that appear nicely quartered.

Many gardeners are not initially attracted to the five-petaled (single) rose because it appears too simple and unadorned. In fact, some even consider species roses not very attractive and rather inferior for use in the home garden. Most people have to cultivate a taste for them. Often gardeners who develop a desire to grow these roses start with the hybrid teas. Then, as their tastes evolve, they may move on to the puffy, many-petaled colorful blooms of the old garden roses, and then perhaps to the species. Species roses and their hybrids are undemanding and easily cared for. However, it is critical to remember that most species are rampant growers. Matching the site to the rose is important; otherwise, a perfectly good shrub suddenly becomes a high-maintenance character—definitely something you want to avoid, particularly in a smaller garden.

Species roses are tough, prickly, deciduous shrubs. For gardeners in cold climates, there are many hardy choices. Blooms are usually single or in clusters, fragrant, and they flower for a few weeks in summer. While more than half of the varieties occur in shades of pink, the remainder run the gamut from white to yellow to dark red. Large and aggressive varieties can be used as ground covers, will scramble up trees, may hide unsightly garages or garden sheds, and climb fences and provide privacy from neighbors—at least for the warmer half of the year while the leaves remain on the canes. Shorter varieties are appropriate for smaller gardens, provided the homeowner tends to their suckering habit (see "Suckering Situations" on p. 21). As colder weather approaches, most species roses develop attractive, colorful hips that extend the season of interest in the garden. Gardeners can leave the hips on the plant until the birds fill their hungry tummies, until they naturally fall off, or until one tires of their bedraggled, prunelike appearance and cuts them off. During the winter, I'll cut hip-filled rose branches and make an arrangement of them with ornamental grasses and other dried plant material dressed with interesting seed heads. The tan plumes of the grasses and the wrinkled, dark reddish hips look attractive together.

Among the more than two hundred species roses, there is wide diversity. Some are big, such as *Rosa filipes,* while others, *R. blanda* for instance, remain under three feet. I chuckle to myself when I think of *R. filipes* and how I first came upon it. It was early spring and, as usual, I was attending the annual plant sale at the Denver Botanic Gardens, roaming through the herbs, vegetables, and rock garden plants, on the prowl for something rare and wonderful. From a distance, I saw a table chockful of roses in gallon containers. Other eager gardeners were clamoring to get to certain ones. I was able to grab *R. sericea pteracantha* (discussed later), a variety for which I had been pining. Hoping to find something more, I continued to search. Suddenly, from behind the counter, a nurseryman pulled out a pot, saying, "Here is *Rosa filipes,* a species."The nurseryman said it would get large. At that moment, his caution didn't concern me. I was simply on the lookout for more roses, especially unusual ones that I hadn't heard of before, varieties difficult to find locally. With its three-foot trailing stem, this species rose looked quite large already, an indication of its future performance. Of course, I grabbed it, thinking I would research it later. Colleagues and friends in the area laughed, knowing my garden was already packed to the brim with roses. But many greedy gardeners, without a moment's hesitation, can always fit in one more prized plant, no matter how stuffed their garden. If push comes to shove, I'll remove a less desirable plant to install something new. I placed these roses in my wobbly grocery cart and headed to the checkout stand, feeling pleased. The canes on *R. filipes* were so long that I had to be cautious as I maneuvered the cart through the crowds of eager garden shoppers—otherwise I would have surely poked a patron with the sharp hooked thorns so abundant along the canes.

When I arrived home, I delved into my library, feeling like an international traveler as I learned more about the background of *R. filipes*. First introduced into commerce in 1908, the hybrid variety I have is called 'Kiftsgate.' It forms huge, loose bunches of creamy white flowers with frilly yellow centers. When in full bloom, it is a spectacular sight and is also blessed with a lush perfume. If left to its own devices, this beauty is a wild rambler that could overtake large portions of my landscape. Thus, I keep a close eye on it as I train it up a fence along my property line. Its origins in western China may signal a lack of hardiness in my region. But my specimen is in a sheltered spot, so it may be protected enough to survive. Time will tell. My attitude toward plants is definitely to favor those that pass the "survival of the fittest" test. In my laidback gardening approach, I'll throw a few shovelfuls of compost over a plant to help it survive our erratic winters. That is all the extra care I'll give it. Even if the 'Kiftsgate' doesn't become a tall climbing shrub, I'm hoping that it will last for a few years as a small shrub rose.

Rosa sericea pteracantha is the other rose I picked up along with 'Kiftsgate'. It had been ten years since I first read about this rose in a magazine where the colored photo of it alone, showing its startling large ruby red thorns, caught my eye immediately. The curved-like-an-archery-bow thorns seemed to climb and wind to the tips of the flower. I could wax poetic about all the attributes of this rose. But after some research and talking with fellow rose "nuts" who had tried to grow this rose in our unpredictable weather and low winter temperatures without success, I came to the sad conclusion that growing *R. sericea pteracantha* would be futile. I planted the rose anyway, only to find it brown and quite dead the following season—even after I mulched it and gave it extra water. Passionate gardeners are no doubt familiar with the tendency to stretch the limits of our gardening zones just a little too far. We pretend a certain plant will survive our climate and are often surprised when it dies. I think I was smart to throw in the towel with this rose. There are hundreds of hardier roses to satisfy my rose cravings.

A widely distributed species rose that needs minimal care is *R. blanda*, which is native to the East Coast and to parts of the western and central United States. I've been growing it for six years and am quite pleased with the results. Covered sparsely with thorns, this spring-blooming rose has small, single, medium-pink flowers. (Technically speaking, roses have bristles, prickles, or both; true thorns, as described in botanical terms, do not appear on roses.) In late summer, round, reddish-green hips appear; they gradually become completely shiny like marble-sized apples and are complemented by a companion planting of *Rudbeckia fulgida* var. *sullivantii* 'Goldsturm' ('Goldsturm' black-eyed Susan), with its abundant yellow daisy flowers, and *Echinacea purpurea* (purple coneflower), covered with drooping pinkish petals with prickly, dark orange centers. When the weather cools even more, the entire rosebush blazes with tints of red and purple. Before a strong snow flattens the area, the yellow daisy *Helianthus salicifolius* 'First Light' (willowleaf sunflower), which at a height of three feet is quite majestic, blooms profusely along the length of its stalk. Encircling the base of this rose is a favorite annual of mine, *Verbena speciosa* 'Imagination'. This low-growing verbena, adorned with button-sized purple flowers, remains attractive well into fall. After all the leaves have fallen off the rose, its twiggy stems are colored deep raspberry red and stand out prominently in the winter landscape.

Suckering Situations

Many species roses, including *Rosa blanda*, sucker profusely. This suckering growth habit has turned some people off to growing roses of any kind. Let me set the record straight. There are two kinds of suckering rose roots; the first is usually undesirable, and the second depends on the viewpoint of the gardener. Let's look at the undesirable habit first. A branch or shoot of a particular rose—the one you may eventually want to buy at the nursery—is grafted onto a hardy rootstock variety, such as *R. canina* or *R. multiflora*. When the grafting process is completed, a bud union exists between two parts. Over time, they fuse and begin to grow as a single plant. Many roses are grown in this fashion, including hybrid teas and floribundas. However, sometimes problems arise. For instance, if a yellow rose has been grafted onto the rootstock of *R. multiflora*, it may grow well for a while. But suddenly, because of harsh winter conditions, insufficient mulching over winter, or lack of adequate moisture, the yellow rose dies and the following spring, a new velvety red rose sprouts, surprising the naïve rose grower. This is a sucker that survived the winter and that now thrives with blooms of white, pink, or red—often not exactly pleasing the gardener who wants yellow. This sucker is the almost-indestructible rootstock of *R. canina* or *R. multiflora*. Because of the death of the grafted variety, the hardy rose beneath will now prevail.

A blistering winter is not the only factor that contributes to the death of a grafted rose. Suckers may appear at other times during the growing season. As soon as the gardener notices atypical shoots extending from any portion of the plant that is below the bud union (a swelling on the "neck" or "stem" of the rose, above the roots, where the rose variety was budded onto the rootstock), she should remove the suckers because they sap energy from the more desired rose and, over time, may eventually kill it. These sprouts often grow a short distance from the base of the rose. If the suckering rootstock is left for a few weeks to mature, it will usually be obvious, upon close examination of the shape and color of the leaves and prickles, that this "new" rose is far different from the rose initially planted. Sometimes novice gardeners need to wait until the rose blooms to see that it differs from their original planted rose. To decipher which rose is which and then to dig down, untangle the roots, and cut or pull the sucker away from the desired rose, as some books recommend, is often a challenge even to the most experienced gardener. My recommendation is to trace these suckers back to their beginning and then cut them off as close to ground level as possible. You may have to repeat this cutting once or twice through the season to discourage suckers.

To prevent death by freezing, it is generally recommended that the bud union of a grafted rose be protected from the cold, especially if there is a lack of sufficient snow cover, a common occurrence in some states. One method is to bury the bud union up to six inches below ground level when planting the rose. However, tender roses such as hybrid teas and floribundas may still die back to the ground, and the experts feel that what grows back from beneath the ground is an inferior-looking plant. Other methods of protection, such as wrapping in styrofoam or the Minnesota Tip Method (which involves digging up the bush and burying it in a trench for the winter), may require too much work or expense to appeal to the average gardener. I prefer to plant roses that remain hardy without special protection, other than a little soil mounding for the first few years.

Another reason for planting a grafted rose with the bud union below ground level is to convert your grafted rose to an "own-root" rose, discussed next. Burying the canes of the desired rose below ground level may stimulate root formation from these canes at or near the graft point. Thus, the rose will grow on its own roots after a while, enhancing its ability to survive a freeze. Some experts claim that planting a grafted rose with the bud union 6 inches below the ground works best, while other experts say 3 to 4 inches in depth is sufficient. Opinions vary. I have not tried this technique, so I cannot vouch for its success. Some gardeners in my area have planted the hybrid tea roses 'Mr. Lincoln' or 'Helen Traubel' and now, twenty-five years later, these roses are still alive and blooming well! It is unclear to me whether this is because they were planted deep, are in a protected spot, or were given extra winter protection. The answer might be a combination of these. (My planting style is discussed in detail in Chapter Six.) Gardening with roses, like other gardening activities, is

not an exact science. Whether a rose lives or dies cannot always be explained simply.

Green leaves snuggle around the light pink blooms of 'Corylus' rose.

The second type of suckering occurs when roses are grown on their own roots (own-root roses), which means they are propagated directly on a cutting from the rose. (Technically speaking, these are not suckers but are runners that spread out underground from the parent plant.) This kind of suckering can be looked at from two different angles. For instance, 'Corylus', a modern, repeat-blooming rose, produces medium-pink, saucer-shaped single flowers. When suckers appear from the base of this rose, unlike suckers on budded varieties, *they will be exactly the same as the mother plant*—medium-pink, saucer-shaped single flowers. These suckers are desirable if you want to make a hedge, expand the overall mass of the rose, move the suckering rose to another place in your garden, or give it away to admiring friends. However, more is not always best. Perhaps your garden space is limited or the rose's suckering habit leads it to encroach on neighboring plants that you cherish. In this particular case, even

When weather cools in fall, the narrow leaves of 'Corylus' rose turn glossy shades of red and orange.

though you'd get more of the exact same roses at no cost, if they do not fit your garden plan, they need to be eliminated.

Experiment to see which approach works best for you: grafted or own-root rose. I try to make sure I purchase roses that are grown on their own roots because they usually live longer than grafted roses and, if they sucker, I am getting the exact same rose that I initially planted. In addition, there is less worry about losing the rose over winter because even if canes are killed to ground level, the underground portion of the plant usually survives and regenerates. However—and there are always exceptions—if I see a rose that I must have and the nursery only offers it grafted, I will buy it and try to remember to bury the roots extra deep, mulch well over winter, and hope that the bud union survives.

More Species

A species rose I would definitely not plant in a small or medium-sized garden is *Rosa multiflora*, because tending the suckers of this rambunctious rose can be quite daunting. *R. multiflora* arches as it curves and claws its way throughout a portion of my backyard garden. Intuitively, I must have guessed that this rose gets gigantic because I planted it in a far corner. Eventually *R. multiflora* will be eliminated from this space to make way for more choice specimens. For now, I tackle this rose patch with strong pruners and loppers and do my every-other-year aggressive stem removal regime so I can still enjoy its fragrant blast of single white flowers in late spring. When the heat subsides in summer, I ruthlessly cut out many suckers. Fortunately, the rose is not too thorny. I was not pleased, however, when the suckers invaded *Acer grandidentatum* (bigtooth maple), a western native that I have been nursing along for six years and that is adorned with stunning red foliage in fall. This maple has been slow to establish itself (it can take seven years or more), so I want to give it all the room it requires rather than having it crowded by an aggressive rose.

The delicate flowers of *Rosa multiflora* bloom in small clusters against a backdrop of greenery.

A rare find I picked up a while back is *R. pulverulenta*. This small-leafed species from southeastern Europe and western Asia is a relative of *R. canina*. However, it does not grow extremely large or wander around my property like *R. canina* and *R. multiflora* would if I let them. For the past seven years, it has remained where I planted it in one of my rock gardens. Most rock gardens are made up completely of small plants. Since I like diversity in my gardens, occasionally I add large, distinctive plants such as *R. pulverulenta* for visual accent. This species has aromatic pine-scented foliage, especially on the new growth, which is plum-colored. Tucked between two large red and black granite boulders, this vase-shaped, 4-foot shrub has single, clear pink blooms in spring. It is not a profuse bloomer for me. The foliage, flowers, and the rugged boulders form an appealing background for the patchwork of rock garden plants below. According to rose expert Martyn Rix, there are at least two forms of *R. pulverulenta*. One is the variety between my rocks. Another form is a smaller, denser one, about 2 feet high and wide, also with single pink flowers. This variety produces masses of attractive, pea-sized red hips in fall that practically engulf the bush and rival the beauty of the single pink flowers that bloom in late spring or early summer.

I am particularly fond of the species *R. spinosissima*. "Spinosissima" means "most thorny," and this is quite apparent in its reddish bristles and prickles. Its half-dollar–sized white flowers have pronounced yellow stamens. These fragrant blooms practically smother this rose for three or four weeks from May into June, so much so that the thin canes bend downward from the sheer weight of the flowers. In fall, the foliage glimmers burnt orange and russet on the mahogany stems and there are a few small bead-sized black hips.

Spinosissimas have been in existence since the Middle Ages. Through them, I feel linked to ancient times. I have been growing mine for more than a decade. *Spinosissimas* were so popular in the early 1800s that, according to Stephen Scanniello and Tania Bayard's book *Roses of America*, in 1831 a bouquet of fifty-five types won an award in the Massachusetts Horticultural Society flower show. Although native to England and Scotland, this rose is extremely hardy, and varieties grow from Iceland to eastern Siberia, as well as

Sweet briar rose, *Rosa spinosissima*, with graceful arching canes, is smothered with blooms in May.

in Europe. In certain places it may grow only 9 inches, while in other spots it reaches 6 feet. In my garden, it is 5 feet high and 4 feet wide. Eventually, it does produce an abundance of suckers; but this rose is near a walkway, so access is easy and it is simple to dispose of or give away plants. The foliage on *R. spinosissima* is dainty, with leaves only ½-inch long.

R. s. altaica, from the Altai Mountains in Siberia, a related variety whose single flowers are a creamy ivory with yellow stamens, has larger black hips that resemble plump Bing cherries. Fellow gardeners have snacked on these hips and commented on how tasty they are. (A colleague told me that once, while teaching about roses, someone in the audience told her she makes fruit leather from ripened rose hips!) If you plant either of these roses, an excellent companion shrub would be any variety of dark purple lilac, such as 'Adelaide Dunbar'. Lilacs often bloom at the same time as the rose, have similar low-water needs, and contrast well with the delicate flowers of the rose. In the Denver area, I was thrilled to see *R. spinosissima altaica* sprouting between cracks in the concrete along alleyways! If you grow this rose in a slightly shaded spot, try pairing it with the perennial *Lamium maculatum* 'White Nancy' (spotted dead nettle). This popular variegated white and green ground cover, with white flowers in spring, is an ideal mate when the rose gently bends, resting its canes and flowers atop 'White Nancy' to create a tapestry of texture and color.

Recently, I acquired a few feet of ground from my neighbors, close to where this rose grows. Aware that I was an insatiable gardener, they said I could plant whatever I wanted to in that spot. I was delighted with this great opportunity. Immediately, I thought of ornamental grasses. Old garden roses, species, and many shrub roses combine superbly with ornamental grasses, because the narrow lines of the grasses provide an appealing contrast to the various leaf sizes of roses. The grasses also mingle attractively with the colorful globular shapes of the blossoms, especially those that bloom into fall.

That same season, once the area was cleaned out, I dug in a small amount of rich compost and planted *Miscanthus sinensis* 'Morning Light' a few feet from *R. spinosissima*. 'Morning Light' is among more than seventy different cultivars of *Miscanthus*, and this is one of the best choices. It has slender foliage and a dome-like round form that will reach 5 feet high and just as wide. An added perk to the beauty of this grass is the white variegation visible on its leaf margins. It blooms late in fall with reddish plumes at the top foot of the plant. This grass, which will be established in about three years, will look elegant as the stems of *R. spinosissima*, with its small black hips, bend and cross through the narrow grass leaves. To fill in open spots along the edges of this new bed, and also to get unusual early spring color, I planted a darling violet: *Viola cornuta* 'Rebecca' ('Rebecca' violet). This ground-cover perennial for shady sites blooms sporadically until fall and has three wavy petals, with a face splashed purple, white, and yellow.

I can't resist planting an ornamental grass whenever I have a rose that is itching for companionship. It's always hard to fathom that a puny grass with only four or five skinny stems in its bleak, black plastic pot can eventually, with patience from the gardener, mature into a beautiful and breathtaking specimen. Within a few feet of the 'Charles de Mills' rose (not a species, but a Gallica, discussed in Chapter Two) I grow *Miscanthus s.* 'Silberfeder' (silver feather). The common name refers to the plant's feathery plumes, which emerge like silvery-white fans with just a slight touch of pink. These inflorescences reach high above the foliage and sometimes droop from the intensity of the sun. However, this graceful habit does not detract from the beauty of the grass. In fact, when the plumes gently cascade into the foliage of the nearby magenta-colored rose, it's a restful and pleasing sight.

A species that I've given freely to colleagues and friends is *R. wichurana* thornless. A sport (a naturally occurring plant variation that arises by spontaneous mutation, and which departs distinctly from normal characteristics of a particular plant), this rose appeared spontaneously in the mid-1960s, at a nursery in Princeton, New Jersey. A thornless variety is uncommon among this species, as many *wichuranas* are known for their menacing hooked thorns. A thornless rose can be put to good use. For instance, it makes an excellent ground cover. To create a beautiful area of ground cover where you currently have grass, follow these steps:

1. Spray grass with an easy-to-use grass killer and wait until the color changes to brown and it is completely dead. With a sharp shovel, turn the clumps over. No compost is needed.

2. Next, pop in small pieces of *R. wichurana*, which root extremely easily. The pliable pencil-thin canes of this rose will coil around the ground and in a few short years, you will have huge sweeps of fragrant white, five-petaled flowers in midsummer, plus a dense semievergreen blanket of green the rest of the year.

Because of this variety's lack of thorns, it is easy to weed. The dense growth of this rose also makes it useful for erosion control of embankments and difficult rocky sites, which tend to wash out when there are blasts of rain in spring or summer. This approach has worked in my garden. The rose is planted on an incline, and the long stems appear to slither along the pea gravel path. When its flowers appear, I watch as the bees attack this rose with gusto.

No matter how I care for or neglect *R. glauca* (syn. *R. rubrifolia*) (red-leaf rose), this species carries on beautifully. Once established, it has been known to do well with only 7 inches of moisture annually.

Sometimes known as the memorial rose because of its frequent use in cemeteries, *Rosa wichurana* contrasts nicely with the blue flowers of *Echinops bannaticus* 'Taplow Blue' (globe thistle).

Dating from the early 1800s, it is famous not only for its perseverance but also for its texture and color. It is exceptionally hardy, reaching about 6 feet high and 5 feet wide, with an outward curve toward the top of the canes. The plum-colored leaves—a highlight of this plant—are about an inch long and cover the shrub from spring to fall. In partially shaded sites, the leaf coloring is more gray-green, but still has dark-colored tints. The reddish-maroon stems on the new growth enhance its overall beauty as well. The five-petaled flat flowers are lilac-pink, becoming white near the light yellow centers. As fall light shines on my landscape, reddish pea-sized hips appear in bunches.

In my novice years of gardening, I overwatered this rose, unaware of its low water needs and wrongly believing that additional water fixes all garden ailments. Sadly, *R. glauca* went to plant heaven! However, a few years later, to my surprise and delight, this indestructible rose reappeared and is now quite content where it was originally planted. In fact, it has sent up seedlings throughout my garden. I dig up these small sprouts and tuck them in here and there, wherever the distinctive features of this rose will punctuate my garden.

Top left: The red-leaf rose (*Rosa glauca*, syn. *R. rubrifolia*) is distinctive alongside its reddish-bronze foliage. (Photo courtesy of Martea A. Graham.)

Top right: As autumn settles in, the shiny rose hips on the red-leaf rose (*Rosa glauca,* syn. *R. rubrifolia*) turn shades of red to burgundy and blend well next to black-eyed Susan.

Left: With a smattering of blooms, the deep burgundy leaves of the statuesque red-leaf rose (*Rosa glauca,* syn. *R. rubrifolia*) truly stand out.

The Persian yellow rose (*Rosa foetida persiana*) is showy next to *Centaurea montana*.

Although I haven't dug up and spread the suckers of *Rosa foetida persiana* (Persian yellow) around, I do enjoy this yellow rose. *R. f. persiana* spontaneously appeared in 1833 in England, possibly originating in Iran (formerly Persia), according to rose historian and expert rose grower Brent C. Dickerson, author of *The Old Rose Adventurer*. Other experts believe Persian yellow was introduced in England via India. This rose has double, tight, globular yellow flowers about the size of small round lemons. It is related to *R. foetida* and its sport, *R. foetida bicolor* ('Austrian Copper'). The former is a single yellow, and as the Latin name *"foetida"* claims, it stinks, although some people like the scent.

I have secured Persian yellow against a fence bordering my property. It contributes a nice touch of structure throughout the seasons, acting as a backdrop to this perennial and shrub border. Every three or four years, in late winter, I'll cut out a few old canes to help rejuvenate its performance. Rose experts recommend pruning one-time bloomers shortly after they finish blooming, usually in July. This is an option that allows sufficient time for newly stimulated growth to

ripen and bloom the following year. But since I garden on my own timetable, rarely adhering to anybody else's rules or schedule, I prune this rose, along with many others, in February or March—or whenever else it suits me. I have more time in winter and can move at a slower pace compared to the frenzy of spring and summer. The plant's structure is more readily visible when not in leaf, making pruning decisions easier. While I may sacrifice some blooms for the current season, in a year or two the shrub will rejuvenate itself and be lush and full again. In addition, many other roses in my garden will pick up any slack if a particular rose is not perky for one year.

'Austrian Copper' has a glitzy, fiery orange color on top and the reverse side is yellow. Its flowers sometimes revert to all yellow. Orange and yellow flowers may appear on the plant at the same time, creating a lovely effect. The growth habit on these two yellow roses is somewhat erect, to about 6 feet, but also can be considered vase-shaped. There is not much winterkill on the canes, and suckering is not a big problem. However, 'Austrian Copper' is a turnoff to some people because its canes have a wiry, unkempt appearance. This flaw can be hidden to some extent by growing various perennials or shrubs nearby. I especially like to use large globular-flowered plants such as *Allium* 'Gladiator' or *Allium aflatunense*, which in some years bloom at the same time as the rose. The first allium has dense florets colored lavender-

Species Roses and Their Hybrids 🌸 33

blue; the sphere of the second one is more lilac-purple. Both grow between 3 and 4 feet and look like floating baseball-sized balloons as they surround this rose. An excellent perennial to plant near 'Austrian Copper' is *Baptisia australis* (blue false indigo). Like the rose, this perennial will last for years with practically no care. The 4-by-4-foot plant has erect branching stems. The top 8 inches are smothered with deep blue flowers, followed in fall by attractive dark-colored seedpods. I'm sentimentally attached to mine since it was one of the first perennials I planted early in my gardening career.

Other plants also serve as good companions to nestle around the base of these yellow roses. First are peonies, darlings of those who dig in the earth. Low-maintenance peonies consort beautifully with a wide variety of plants. A few well-placed plants will cover up the gangly brown canes of the roses. Although in most gardens peonies bloom after the roses, their foliage provides a nice evergreen appearance. If fall weather holds, without early major snows, the pointy leaves of the peony often turn maroon, adding brightness as cool weather approaches.

Another plant I have grown near these yellow roses is *Salvia buchananii*. An annual, this salvia gives a showy performance. At about 15 inches in height, it has inch-long glossy dark green leaves. Its velvety rich raspberry-red tubular flowers remind me of penstemons (beard tongue), which also have tongue-like flowers. Even though this plant won't cover up all of the rose canes, I guarantee you'll be glad you bought it!

Salvia buchananii, as well as other salvias with pointy purplish flowers, such as *S. sclarea* (clary sage) and *S. pratensis*, would also pair well with the fragrant double blooms of 'Harison's Yellow'. After several years—perhaps four or five—both of these salvias may need to be thinned so as not to take over a flower bed. I mistakenly installed 'Harison's Yellow'—a thorny 6-foot rose—too close to a path. But I have left it there because it acts as a beautiful background to my rock garden, which is packed with a host of large and small plants. Some, such as *Papaver triniifolium* (Armenian poppy), can be seen from afar. Its papery thin peachy-salmon flowers make a great match with the yellow rose in back. I have let this biennial, which reaches about 3 feet, seed itself throughout my garden. I have done the same with the blue flowers of *Consolida ambigua* (annual larkspur). A plant that adds more height among the rocks and the rose is *Verbascum bombyciferum* 'Arctic Summer' (mullein). The plant's rocketlike stems, with their woolly white appearance, are clothed in a profusion of butter-yellow flowers. At the base of the stem is a large, soft silvery rosette of leaves, up to 18 inches in width, which also adds texture to this planting. As I stroll closer to this area, I delight in seeing an unknown, loud crimson dianthus at my feet. I imagine I am Gretel, delightfully lost in a forest of flowers and wondering which way to go!

'Harison's Yellow' suckers profusely. Several times in summer or winter I grab a strong pair of loppers, sharp pruners, and a comfy cushion, then settle into cutting down all the extra shoots that get in my way when I work in this area or walk from one section of my garden to another.

Another yellow species (and one that I planted in a perfect spot, giving it all the room it desires) is *Rosa hugonis* 'Father Hugo'. This monster of a rose has reached almost 6 feet high and wide in

The Golden Rose of China (*Rosa hugonis* 'Father Hugo') mingles with the grayish foliage of four-wing saltbush (*Atriplex canescens*).

just three years. I'm not too impressed with its single-cupped flowers, which last barely a week in my garden, but I am attracted to its fernlike foliage that turns reddish in the fall, as well as to its vaselike shape. Famous among rosarians, it is commonly known as the Golden Rose of China, or 'Father Hugo' rose, after Reverend Hugh Scallan, who discovered it in China in 1899. A fast grower, this rose needs pruning every other year, otherwise it becomes too dense and does not look so attractive. Next to it, and to complement the prickly habit and tiny leaves of the rose, is the reseeding annual *Datura meteloides* (angel's trumpet), known for its large pointed green leaves, as well as its smooth purple-red stems. I love its highly fragrant white flowers. If you have young children in your garden, it is important to remember that the seeds and flowers of this plant are poisonous.

In many years, I've been fortunate to have a rose bloom in late April. This unique early-blooming rose arrived in my garden serendipitously. Years ago, while browsing the Denver Botanic Gardens' Rock Alpine Garden, a colleague offered me a small 4-inch pot with *Rosa hemisphaerica* (syn. *R. rapinii*) tucked in. The rose languished: it needed to be planted soon, or otherwise it might die. My colleague had no time to plant it. In addition, he was more than well stocked with plants—and not being a rose person, he handed this gem off to me, knowing I would give it a good home. I did just that, watering and nursing it along for several years. I did some research as well and learned this species is native to parts of Turkey and Iran. Today this single yellow rose, with a light scent, is 4 feet tall and almost as wide. The leaves are finely textured and turn shades of bronzy red in fall. Sometimes it is sparsely covered with red hips. This rose has a lovely vase shape. Since it is such an early bloomer, its blossoms create beautiful scenes near various rock garden plants that also bloom early. For instance, it flowers in concert with the dangling pink blossoms of prairie smoke (*Geum triflorum*).

A final yellow species that can stand alone and look magnificent is *Rosa xanthina*. Its bright yellow, somewhat cupped flowers appear in late spring to early summer. Its growth habit is upright and the rose eventually reaches 5 feet. I grew this rose for a number of years but, sadly, I crowded it with neighboring plants until it finally

disappeared. Species, like many other roses, need room to stretch out their canes and mature. There is a fine line to draw between two concepts: Is the rose planted too close to surrounding plants, which might inhibit its growth potential and make it more susceptible to disease, or do these plants complement the all-embracing beauty of the rose and still give it enough room to shine? Judging this requires knowledge, common sense, experience gained through trial and error, and awareness of one's personal style.

I'll always keep 'Stanwell Perpetual', a frilly, pale pink fragrant rose that appeared by chance in the nineteenth century in Stanwell, England. The *spinosissima* blood in its background explains its fernlike foliage. Its northern heritage makes 'Stanwell Perpetual' an excellent hardy choice for gardeners in cold climates. I purchased my plant by mail order a number of years ago from a nursery in the Northeast. While the catalog stated the rose would grow to 5 feet, in the semi-arid Rocky Mountain region plants often achieve smaller stature than claimed in catalogs that originate from the East or West Coast.

The nodding, pink blossoms of prairie smoke (*Geum triflorum*) get a perk when the cupped, yellow flowers of *Rosa hemisphaerica* bend nearby.

Initially I planted 'Stanwell Perpetual' toward the back of a border, expecting a 5-foot shrub. But this twiggy bush never grew that big, remaining at 3 feet high and wide. As I roamed my garden from summertime into fall when it bloomed—a two- or three-month blooming period—I always had to walk around the few plants behind which it was hidden to see its full blush-pink blooms, as well as to relish its deliciously intense fragrance. Finally, I moved it to where it is much more visible and a pleasure to enjoy. Once a year in late winter or early spring, it is a good idea to prune this rose down to a foot or so. Because of its twiggy growth habit, this technique will help keep the plant compact and blooming well.

In keeping with the gray-green foliage of the 'Stanwell Perpetual' and to bring out more gray in the mix, I planted it near the Colorado native *Atriplex confertifolia* (shadscale saltbush). This silvery, dense shrub with a round growth habit will eventually reach 3 to 4 feet high and wide. It blooms in the summertime—the same time as 'Stanwell Perpetual'—with sulfur yellow flowers and unique rugged tan and thorny branches. Although from divergent habitats, these plants will be a perfect pair for years to come. Daring gardeners who want to add flare to this rosy scene might try *Sphaeralcea munroana* (Munro's globe mallow), also tolerant of dry conditions. This medium-sized perennial that grows 2 to 3 feet tall has coral-red, saucer-shaped flowers with matte green leaves.

A rose that needs a moister spot is 'Metis', descendant of the wild *Rosa nitida*, native to the East Coast. 'Metis' has a lax but attractive growth habit that mingles easily among perennials and other shrubs. The flower has five petals and is bubblegum pink, with a touch of yellow in the center. Aside from having to do a late winter cleanup and thinning out a few unkempt stems now and then, I've rarely been bothered with much suckering or winterkill. I like the plant's thin reddish canes, which have minimal thorns on the new growth and also on the mid-aged stems. As the plant matures, the canes become masses of slender prickles and bristles. The small, dark, glossy green leaves turn scarlet in autumn. With its distinctive fall foliage color, 'Metis' combines well with three perennials in the area: *Sedum* 'Autumn Joy' (stonecrop), a common favorite with pink flowers; *Geranium* 'Patricia' (cranesbill), topped like a canopy with large magenta flowers marked with a dark star-shaped eye; and the popular *Rudbeckia triloba* (three-lobed coneflower), known for its almost-black center eye. Three-lobed coneflower self-sows prolifically in my garden.

For some reason, *Rosa moyesii* has not performed well for me. It has been a bit overcrowded, but this season I've diligently cleaned up around it, allowing more air and sunshine to penetrate the bed. Next spring I hope to see its dark red single blooms arranged in small groups. *R. moyesii* is famous for its bright orange-red hips. An excellent variety of *R. moyesii* is 'Geranium'. This past spring, I planted

For autumn color, the foliage of *Rosa nitida* is sensational, especially juxtaposed with the yellow flowers of black-eyed Susan (*Rudbeckia triloba*).

one (and am giving it room) so it will reach its potential of about 5 feet in my region. 'Geranium' is one of the most famous *moyesii* hybrids because its single flowers are geranium red. In addition, it is prized for the oblong red fruit it produces in fall.

Another famous *moyesii* is 'Nevada', bred initially in Spain in the 1920s. When I first became infatuated with roses, 'Nevada' immediately charmed me with its vivacious floral display. A majestic shrub, it reaches at least 6 feet, with a similar spread. 'Nevada' begins its rise to stardom with somewhat fat, pinkish buds, which open to 4-inch wide, creamy white fragrant flowers. Its loose and informal semidouble blooms appear first in late spring in such profusion that they nearly obscure the light green foliage. 'Nevada' gives a repeat performance intermittently in summer and fall. Thorns are sparse on the wide-arching chocolate brown canes, making it an appealing choice for gardeners who like roses but dislike their prickly ways. When I first saw this shrub at a friend's house, she had it planted near 'Harison's Yellow'. The yellow and white flowers, like brass cymbals clashing together in a marching band, created a potent scene. Beneath these shrubs, she dressed the ground with masses of *Geranium* 'Johnson's Blue', which was a nice complement to the rose colors.

Unfortunately, I have killed this rose at least twice, and I'm about to give up on it totally. I don't know exactly what the problem is. Perhaps, in its early years it needed a bit of coddling or extra water or more winter protection. Maybe I'll just have to enjoy this rose at my friend's house.

Rugosas

The Rugosas are an exciting group falling under the umbrella of species roses. Rugosas originated in northern China, Japan, and Korea, where they flourished for centuries; historical evidence shows that they date as far back as 1000 A.D. Gradually, over centuries, they were introduced into Europe as well as to North America. In this section, I describe the species or wild roses, such as *Rosa rugosa rubra,* as well as the many beautiful hybrids that have been developed over the past hundred years or so. (Theoretically speaking, the Rugosa hybrids are considered modern roses because no hybrid form occurred in Europe prior to 1867, the beginning date of hybrid teas, the official cutoff date that sets old garden rose classes apart from modern ones.) The Rugosas have many advantages and a few slight disadvantages. I'll begin with their strengths. An important characteristic is that the flowers repeat bloom, a trait that is highly uncommon for species roses, and one that gardeners appreciate. These roses are tough as nails, known to be hardy to minus 50 degrees. These two features alone are enough to make them desirable for gardeners in harsh climates. Another unique asset is their foliage, which, on most of these roses, is somewhat thick and wrinkly, quite different from many other roses with smoother textures. Usually resistant to disease, species Rugosas are excellent for gardeners who want no-fuss or low-maintenance gardening. However, recently I noticed large walnut-sized balls appearing on a few of my Rugosas. I learned this is crown gall, a bacterial disease that attacks ornamental shrubs, roses, and vines. I hope to control it by cutting out all the dead cane and the gall whenever I spot it.

Whether you prefer single flowers or full, blousy blooms, or anything in between, there is definitely a Rugosa rose to your liking. Blossoms come in purple-crimson, light and dark pink, reds, pure white, and yellow. Depending on soil condition, location, and the moisture they receive, they can range in height from 2 to 6 feet.

I have grown *Rosa rugosa alba* for a long time. It snuggles near a fence along a woodland path, so I can easily inhale its heavenly scent, which in my opinion is one of the best in the world of roses. I compare it to the strong perfume of irises. I love to poke my nose into both of these delicious flowers. The rose reaches 3 feet high and wide, with new shoots always coming from its base. The closed buds are pale pink and unfurl to reveal 3-inch single-cupped white flowers adorned with coppery yellow stamens. Like most Rugosas, this one repeat blooms and in fall produces large cherry red hips that add a nice ornamental touch through the cold winter months. For added vitality, beneath the rose I have planted a sweep of *Geranium sanguineum* (bloody cranesbill), whose foliage turns Titian red in fall. A few times a year, especially in late winter, as old canes die or break off, I simply cut them down to the

The white blossoms of *Rosa rugosa alba* take center stage around the shrub's dark green leaves.

ground, which encourages new canes to appear. An easy-care rose, with the wrinkled green leaves characteristic of most Rugosas, *R. r. alba* makes an excellent garden subject in full sun or a lightly shaded site. The canes sucker some, but not nearly to the extent of 'Harison's Yellow'.

Not far from *R. r. alba* is its close relative, *R. r. rubra*. This rose is similar in shape to *R. r. alba*, but has slightly cupped magenta flowers, and the stamens are creamy ivory. In fall, as the orange-red hips emerge, I enjoy a few more highly fragrant flowers. I have this rose planted among perennials and other shrubs, such as *Picea pungens* 'Globosa' (globe spruce), with its steely blue foliage. I also enjoy the ground-cover effect *Oenothera macrocarpa* (Ozark sundrop) brings to the décor, with its patches of squarish yellow flowers.

A Rugosa rose that doesn't put out any hips is 'Linda Campbell'. This Rugosa has been around since 1990 and was named after an editor of the American Rose Society publication, *The American Rose Annual*. It is not fragrant, but redeems itself when it repeatedly produces frothy

red flowers with white toward the center. The flowers come in large clusters, more than fifteen buds to each bunch. The flowers have good form as they gradually fade to a darkish pink and then shrivel. I have seen 'Linda Campbell' used successfully at a public rose garden, where eight bushes surrounded a simply adorned gazebo.

This medium-sized shrub with slightly arching branches has been slow to establish itself in my garden because it was previously crowded by other plants. With improved space to grow, I suspect it will eventually mature close to 5 feet high and wide. I've seen this rose do well in quite a shady location, where it stays at about 3 feet high and its canes spread out horizontally among nearby perennials and trees. I've improvised on my design scheme and planted a pot-pourri of plants near 'Linda Campbell'. I use *Cytisus supinus* (broom) and *Eragrostis trichoides* (sand love grass). Brooms are special plants for me; I am attracted to their yellow pealike flowers and easy maintenance. I was lucky to find *C. supinus* at a specialty nursery because, according to local nursery people, it is not widely available. The plant's soft, lime-green foliage will hug the base of the rose. Its flowers appear in June and, when mature, it will reach 2 feet high and spread to 4 feet. The 3-foot sand love grass is vibrant in fall, dressed in dainty reddish-purple inflorescences that turn bronze as winter creeps in.

Left: Rosa rugosa rubra has fluffy, pink blossoms that are a vibrant counterpoint to its wrinkled foliage.

Right: The hips of *Rosa rugosa* are shiny orange or red until a strong frost hits. Then, they wrinkle like a prune!

'Linda Campbell' rose, shrouded in shade, has a velvety, mysterious appearance.

Reddish-pink buds of 'Belle Poitevine' rose bloom to reveal medium-pink flowers.

The plumes gradually become sand colored and finally, as winter truly grips my garden, they are crushed by snow.

One of my favorite Rugosa roses is 'Belle Poitevine'. For about eight years, I have had this Rugosa near my mailbox, where it receives little attention or extra water but thrives nonetheless. The bush makes a thorny mound barely 2 feet high and wide, with little suckering or cane dieback. The bloom is lavender-pink, with an extravagant number of radiant petals. The rose's spicy clove fragrance is heavenly. My neighbor took a sniff of this rose and thinks it smells like champagne. Purchase this rose and see what your nose will call it!

I have used *Lavendula angustifolia* 'Jean Davis' (lavender) as a companion plant with this rose. I like its pinkish-white narrow flower, although its fragrance reminds me of paint thinner! I let this area stay very dry, which keeps 'Jean Davis' to 12 inches high. I also have a few sedums in this area; their reddish tops and succulent green leaves are attractive next to the lavender-pink rose color. In fall, the rose foliage turns rich hues of burgundy and orange. These colors become even more vibrant when the shrub *Prunus besseyi* (western sand cherry) pokes its reddish-brown stems and coppery glossy leaves through the rose canes.

A popular Rugosa hybrid is 'Thérèse Bugnet'. I often find plant names curious, especially those of roses, and wonder how a particular rose got its name. *Botanica's Roses* states that the grower named this rose for a close family member. The bountiful lavender-pink flowers come in clusters of three to five and open with a pleasing sweet scent. Its first flush of bloom in spring is heavy, and it reblooms in summer and fall.

I maintain there are four reasons, aside from its beautiful flowers, for 'Thérèse Bugnet's' popularity. First is its hardiness in colder regions of the country. Developed in Canada more than fifty years ago, this disease-resistant, 5-foot high shrub, with a slight arching growth habit, experiences very little winterkill on the canes. I just need to snip off a few brown tips and shriveled, dark red hips in early May. The second reason for its appeal might be how drought tolerant it is. Once established, 'Thérèse Bugnet' blooms powerfully, requiring only minimal water. Third, gardeners may covet this rose for the few prickles on the stems. Finally, the amazing red-orange foliage of the

Left: 'Thérèse Bugnet' rose is showy against a backdrop of dark green foliage. (Photo courtesy of Marlea A. Graham)

Right: For an intriguing companion near 'Thérèse Bugnet' rose, plant Sicilian onion (*Nectaroscordum siculum*). The hanging florets, colored plum to pink, will attract many onlookers.

leaves and stems is highly desirable, almost rivaling the crimson fall color of *Euonymus alatus* (burning bush). The lingering foliage of 'Thérèse Bugnet' heightens the appeal of the garden during the cooler months, when most herbaceous plants have disappeared or become piles of mush once heavy snows have hit. Near the rose, I planted a statuesque ornamental grass, *Miscanthus sinensis* 'Graziella'. As fall moves into full swing, the fancy, curled off-white plumes of this grass accentuate the vibrant earthy tones of the rose's foliage.

Occasionally, I'll notice that a cane or part of a cane and its leaves have shriveled and turned brown during the growing season. I simply cut away this part of the shrub and let the rest of 'Thérèse Bugnet' shine through. I take this same course of action when this happens to any of my roses, remembering that pruning stimulates new growth and hence more blooms. It also removes any burrowing insect that may be causing the problem.

This rose grows in a bed that combines various large and small perennials and ornamental grasses. At the peak of summer, this area looks pretty jungly. However, I like gardens where all the flowers mingle and touch each other with carefree abandon, like happy relatives enjoying a family reunion.

A long-time member of my Rugosa family of roses is 'Hansa'. I'm quite fond of this shrub both because of its unusual crimson-purple flower and its refreshing spicy clove scent. In my garden it remains under 4 feet and is well-behaved, not suckering around.

As the result of breeders continuing to cross roses with one another, creating varieties with more cold tolerance and disease resistance, the Rugosa family is always expanding. Two Canadian-bred roses, 'Jens Munk' and 'Martin Frobisher', have Rugosa heritage. These roses are part of a group of hardy Canadian roses bred by Dr. Felicitas Svejda known as the "Explorer Series," all bearing the names of famous Canadian explorers.

I have been growing these two Rugosas for a number of years. 'Martin Frobisher' has been around since the late 1960s, when thoughts of roses—or for that matter *any* facet of gardening—did not even flicker in my mind! In my garden, this rose reaches 5 feet tall, with mostly stiff, vertical canes. Some suckering shoots have sprouted: since I liked where they popped up, I decided to leave them. In a few years, I will have a nice grouping. Winter dieback has been modest, which speaks to hardiness in cold climates. The lightly fragrant flowers are double, with about forty petals, and the color is a soothing pale pink touched with lilac. Mature stems are reddish plum and not very thorny, while new growth is light green. If I have any complaint about this rose, it would be that the spent blooms stay on the plant too long and are unkempt in appearance. The remedy is undemanding. I can spiff up my pruning technique and quickly prune off the old blooms. Or when I walk on the path where this rose is located, I can take hold of the dry, aging blooms, crunch them in the palm of my hand, and simply scatter them to the wind. I prefer this latter approach. This rose is not a prolific bloomer. To compensate, place it in a bed with other flowers, so that some of the rose's lower canes, which are not profuse with blooms, can be covered up by surrounding flowers. Despite 'Martin Frobisher's' "stinginess" with regard to flowering, in fall my eyes gravitate to its gently scalloped leaves in snazzy tones of brick-red, apple-green, and chartreuse.

'Jens Munk' has flashy pink double blooms surrounding a butter-yellow center. This vigorous and thorny shrub blooms from

'Hansa' rose has large blossoms accented with a touch of yellow in the center.

The pale pink blooms of 'Martin Frobisher' rose create a striking vignette when combined with *Geranium magnificum*.

The pink flowers of 'Jens Munk' rose nestle among the spiky, lavender shoots of a variety of lamb's ears (*Stachys spicata purpurea*).

June through August and briefly in fall. It has a spicy scent and forms a 4-foot mound. The pink blooms, along with its Rugosa-textured foliage, are exquisite when they bond with the puffy gray foliage of *Artemisia* 'Powis Castle' (sage). Other plants that round out this scene include: *Kniphofia uvaria* (red-hot poker), with its spearlike flower heads mixed orange and yellow, and *Scabiosa ochroleuca* (yellow pincushion flower) with soft yellow flowers and wiry stems that reach 2 feet. To accent the rose in fall, asters are a great pick. I like the blooms of *Aster* x *frikartii* 'Flora's Delight' (Frikart's aster), which produces warm lilac blooms.

Rugosa 'Sir Thomas Lipton', which I have not grown, has received bad press. Suzanne Verrier, author of *Rosa Rugosa* believes this particular rose is a poor representative of Rugosa hybrids. She sees it as ungraceful, having a rigid habit of growth with blooms that are sometimes misshapen, and bearing sparse foliage. Other garden writers have not spoken so harshly about it. In fact, in *Fifty Easy Old-Fashioned Roses, Climbers, and Vines*, Anne M. Zeman praises it for its small white peony-like blossoms, reflexed petals, and typical rugged carefree character. A few friends of mine in the Denver area have tried this rose and are not pleased with its performance, however, due to the sparseness of its flowers and its slow growth. A colleague grows 'Sir Thomas Lipton' and, in spite of the low amount of blooms it produces, he likes it because the plant's abundant thorns deter schoolchildren from stomping on and running over his prized flower beds! An essential point about this rose, as well as most other roses that I describe, is that these roses *need time to get established*. They will not become lush and huge, overflowing with beautiful blossoms, within a mere couple of years of planting, especially in cold climates. Of course, there are always exceptions. My neighbor planted the Canadian rose 'William Baffin', a raspberry-red climber, and in a year it put on 6 feet of growth! Mine was planted at the same time and only put on 2 feet of growth. However, mine received a slight bit less sun than hers. The gardener needs patience, patience, and more patience. As the rose matures, it is getting comfortable, anchoring its roots in the soil. In time, it will produce the vivid flowers and lush green growth that gardeners crave and expect. There isn't an exact timetable. Each rose bush has its particular growth characteristics, reflecting the soil and conditions it is planted in and the amount of sun and water it receives. However, there is a flip side to this story. If, after a certain amount of time (to be determined by you), the rose is not robust and flourishing, it may indicate that the rose is not happy where it is planted or not happy in your garden at all, and it may need to be tossed. If it has grown only 6 inches after three years or has had only one flimsy bloom each year for three consecutive years, then you are holding onto a dream that you should let go of. It is good to know when it is time to rip out a plant, replacing it with something new that is more adaptable.

A Rugosa that I will not be ripping out any time soon is 'Agnes'. The fragrant double blossoms of this rose are pale yellow, with slightly deeper tones toward the center. The blooms are not excessive, but they do cover the bush nicely in early summer and repeat sporadically in the fall. The thick dark green foliage (with no yellowing of the leaves) is heavily crinkled on this prickly 5-foot shrub with erect and bending canes. *Deschampsia cespitosa* (tufted hair grass), a delicate clumping ornamental grass, encircles this rose, providing contrast in foliage. For something different, try growing the annual *Euphorbia marginata* (snow-on-the-mountain). Its whitish-green bracts and smooth leaves create a nice contrast next to 'Agnes' and her thorny leaves. All hardy geraniums—many known for their ravishing rich colors—are superb companions to yellow roses such as 'Agnes'. In this instance, I have used *G. psilostemon*, because I like that it squiggles through plants effortlessly, reaching 4 feet, topped off by cupped maroon flowers, dotted with a dark colored eye.

An impressive Rugosa hybrid to plant adjacent to 'Agnes' is 'Basye's Purple Rose'. I bought a small specimen at a rose conference and then waited four long years before blooms appeared! Since the stems are a rare dark reddish-purple that add texture and color to the landscape, I tolerated the wait. Finally, a few blooms appeared, as beautiful as I had imagined, unparalleled by those of any other rose. The flat, but slightly wavy purplish flowers are more than 2 inches across and veiled in a fruity fragrance. Like most Rugosas, this one repeat-blooms and suckers somewhat, but not a great deal. I won't mind the suckers one bit so I can gush over more of the royal purple color). In addition, I most definitely

With only five petals, the cupped purple flowers of 'Basye's Purple Rose' offer tremendous visual appeal.

will share this rose with other avid gardeners, since sources are not abundant either locally or by mail order. My 3-by-3-foot specimen receives average moisture; since Dr. Basye, who bred this rose in 1980 in Texas, was seeking drought tolerance and hardiness, I suspect this rose would bloom well in a rather dry section of the garden.

The disadvantages of Rugosas are almost insignificant when compared to their assets. Rugosas grow well in most soils; however, in heavy clay they sometimes develop chlorosis, a yellowing of the leaves. The extravagant colors of the flowers don't stand out as well with the yellowed leaves as they would against healthy dark green leaves. If this defect is bothersome, it can usually be remedied somewhat with a few applications of Ironite, a natural granular substance that needs to be worked into the soil. Because I am drawn to attend to the many other tasks in the garden, I ignore the slight discoloration and focus on the exuberant flowers instead.

The scarlet blossoms of 'Robusta' rose become even more vivid when they mix with the summer blossoms of 'Mexican hat' (*Ratibida columnifera*).

As I write this chapter, fall nudges my landscape ever so slowly. Undoubtedly, I will need more roses next season and Rugosas are high on my list, even though their foliage is imperfect and they occasionally get crown gall. I'm browsing catalogs, searching garden Web sites, and flipping through gardening books, looking for vibrant pictures of roses with eloquent descriptions. One I plan to order is 'Robusta'. The name speaks to its plush scarlet flower. It blooms in clusters of five curvy petals and has a light fragrance; its shiny dark green foliage contrasts well with the crimson-colored flower. Even though most Rugosas repeat-bloom, some varieties perform better than others and 'Robusta' has a good track record. In warmer climates, I've seen it used as a climber. But I suspect for northern gardeners it would remain in the 4- to 5-foot range. I look forward to growing this rose.

If you're new to rose gardening or haven't tried a species rose, take a chance and buy one. Although many only bloom once, that one time is often so meaningful that planting them is well worth the small financial investment. Besides, you can feel proud that you are growing a great rose with historical significance.

CHAPTER TWO

The Birth of the Beauties: From Ancient to Modern Roses

HOW DID THE MOSTLY SINGLE-FLOWERED species roses transform into the many-petaled roses that adorn landscapes today? The question cannot be fully or simply answered. For thousands of years, interbreeding in the wild occurred naturally among species. A chance seedling might spontaneously appear with a blossom quite different from the original one, filled with additional petals. But when and how this happened remains a puzzle. In many cases, we can only imagine what occurred. Extensive rose-breeding records were not kept by ancient civilizations. Even in current times, when we know the parents of roses involved in the breeding, sometimes the results are unforeseen and more surprising than we expected. Rose classification is not an exact science, and some latitude must be given in determining to which class a rose belongs and exactly when double forms came about. Aside from species roses, the Gallica roses are generally considered the oldest; traces of Gallicas have been found that date back as early as the twelfth century B.C. when, according to Ann Reilly's book, *The Rose*, the Persians used this rose as a religious symbol. It once bloomed over the entire Mediterranean region and its exact origin remains a mystery.

According to *The Graham Stuart Thomas Rose Book*, the first double rose was recorded in Urania by Herodotus (ca. 440 B.C.). Herodotus writes of a rose found in Macedonia with sixty petals. In addition, Theophrastus, in his systematic classification of all known plants of his time (ca. 300 B.C.), mentions a hundred-petaled rose.

For a period of time after the fall of the Roman Empire, the history of the rose is somewhat vague. However, in the twelfth and thirteenth centuries, the rose surfaced again. As travel became easier, crusaders and traders began exchanging plants, and rose specimens arrived in Europe, thus initiating an early phase of rose cultivation.

These early once-blooming old garden roses have been classified into five categories—Gallicas, Damasks, Albas, Centifolias, and Moss Roses. All of these roses bloom once for a few weeks in early summer and then act as a backdrop for the blooms of other plants. These are the roses that were cultivated in Europe before the introduction of the repeat-blooming roses of Asia, which brought radical change to the rose scene. (Most Rugosas repeat-bloom and are discussed in Chapter One: other repeat-bloomers are discussed in Chapters Four and Five.) Many of the old garden roses from Europe are hardy and perform vigorously for gardeners in harsh climates. They offer varying degrees of fragrance, and colors range from white to shades of pink through dark, vivid colors such as purple and magenta. Their overall shapes are bushy, arching, and compact, and will range in height from 3 to 7 feet. They mix well with other plants and can also stand alone in the landscape as specimen plants, attracting attention as their blooms explode in the garden in early summer. Although I grow many hardy modern roses that repeat-bloom, I will always grow once-blooming roses because of their many attributes, such as attractive rose hips, powerful perfume, and pleasing shape. In addition, I like growing roses whose background is knitted together with ancient civilizations.

Gallica Roses

For gardeners in northern climates, as well as for those who garden in small spaces, Gallica roses are excellent choices. They generally remain under 4 feet, forming bushy, compact shrubs, some with fine prickles, and others with larger thorns. They will sucker, so either let them run or clip them off, whichever suits your fancy. Gallicas adapt to a wide range of soil conditions. They don't need a

lot of soil amending (although there is some debate about this). Some gardeners in areas with hard clay soil do not amend their soil for old garden roses and species roses, and yet they achieve spectacular bloom. Other gardeners claim that the addition of compost improves performance.

Like most roses, the Gallicas do not favor wet feet, so drainage is crucial. Also like most roses, Gallicas crave sun, but will still bloom in partial shade, although not as floriferously. Flower colors of the Gallicas can be dramatic, and include burgundy, violet, and plum, as well as the more common shades of pink. There are even striped or flecked varieties such as 'Camaieux' and the famous 'Rosa Mundi', also known as *Rosa gallica versicolor*. 'Rosa Mundi' appeared sometime in the sixteenth century. Legend claims that it is named after Fair Rosamond, King Henry II's mistress. 'Rosa Mundi', a double form, is clothed in lighter shades of pink, but it is quite distinctive, with the petals splashed pink and white. To complement the scene around these flamboyant roses, grow early blooming varieties of pinks (dianthus) and hardy geraniums.

A Gallica that I was smitten with years ago is 'Alika', also known as *R. gallica grandiflora*, a rose that traveled west from Russia in 1906. I obtained it by mail order in one of those 8-inch packages. It has

Left: With green foliage for contrast in the background, this ancient rose, 'Rosa Mundi', first mentioned in 1581, appears splashed with crimson, pink, and white paint.

Right: The saucer-shaped, crimson blooms of 'Alika' rose are highlighted with yellow stamens and the lavender flowers of big betony (*Stachys grandiflora*).

grown 4 feet high and wide. Because of its suckering abilities, which are fairly strong, I know it will get even wider if I let it have free rein in my garden. Its fragrant crimson blooms have a blousy appearance. In June, the blooms of the 'Alika' are so abundant and the hum of the bees swarming the plant is so intense that Brent C. Dickerson, author of *The Old Rose Adventurer*, heard someone remark that it seemed as though the 'Alika' bush made musical sounds! Highlights of this rose are its pronounced buttery yellow stamens in the center of the bloom, as well as the dark green serrated leaves that gently droop. The hips are shaped like small Hershey's Kisses, and they crinkle as the weather chills. When fall stirs in my garden, I enjoy watching the hips transform on the bush from shades of green to tints of fiery orange and red. In late September, the hips are multicolored—the top half is orange-red and the bottom is lime-green. Before snowy weather comes along and strips the leaves from their grip on the mahogany stems, they form a glimmering mosaic of orange, red, and chocolate shades.

To add showstopping elegance when this rose is in bloom, beneath it I planted a sweep of *Stachys grandiflora* (big betony), a mound-shaped, 1-foot-high perennial with spikelike violet flowers and dark green scalloped leaves. If your mood is mellower, use *Alchemilla mollis* (lady's mantle), with its chartreuse coloring, to soften the overall picture. For additional fall texture and color, in a flower bed across the way, where conditions are drier, I have a few plants of *Chrysothamnus* spp. (rabbitbrush), whose fluffy yellow flowers and gray-green leaves refresh the planting scene.

I must confess I'm a foliage fanatic. I love leaves. Of course I love flowers immensely, especially roses, with their voluptuous colors, but through the years leaves and other plant accents, such as stems and thorns, have captured my attention as well. I'm impressed with the additional effect foliage brings to the garden. Once flowers have finished their long or short magnificent burst of color, foliage remains on plants until it is zapped by winter weather. Foliage textures add spice to the garden. Sometimes I like to observe leaves closely. Their patterns remind me of a detailed street map.

The Gallicas have unique characteristics. At a rose conference a few years back, I purchased 'Hippolyte', mostly because its name

The light green leaves of 'Désirée Parmentier' are a gentle variation next to the full-petaled, lavender-pink blossoms of the rose.

sounded quirky and the distinctive picture taped to the display table tempted me with intense reddish-violet blossoms and handsome foliage. When I arrived home, I quickly tucked it in well and gave it a good drink of water. It has been slow to mature because larger shrubs and perennials blocked out sunlight and air circulation, inhibiting its growth. Since I have cleaned up around it, 'Hippolyte' is thriving. In the future, I will savor its blooms as well as its delectable perfume. While it has grown these last few years, I have been able to better examine its unusual, small, smooth green leaves, which, on new growth in fall, are gently etched deep purple. In addition, this rose is practically thorn free. Although you may buy roses for their beautiful blooms and sweet scents, as you walk around your garden before or after the blooms have finished, pause a moment and observe the attractive greenery.

When I was less knowledgeable about growing roses, and before I paid stricter attention to rose size or had enough beds prepared, I often stuck a rose in the ground quickly just to get it in. (I admit that

Right: The single pink and white blooms of 'Complicata' rose, dotted with a yellow center, have an elegant flair.

Below: 'Complicata' rose is in the company of two rock garden plants. One, the dianthus, echoes the pink in the rose. Beard tongue (*Penstemon pinifolius* 'Mersea Yellow') adds a cheery splash of yellow.

I sometimes still behave in this manner!) I did this with two Gallica roses. First is 'Désirée Parmentier', which is crammed into a small space in my garden. (Debate surrounds the exact identity of this rose. Some experts feel it doesn't fit in with either the Gallicas or the Damasks and therefore, think it needs to be categorized as a "found rose"—meaning a rose whose exact identity is unclear at this time.) It has grown almost 6 feet high and just as wide. Come early spring, I plan to move it to a roomier position in the middle of a mostly shrub border, where it can command all the space it needs. I'll try to plant it close enough to my grassy area so that I can breathe in its heavenly scented blooms and view the rosy pink flowers, which appear tightly coiled with many petals. 'Désirée Parmentier' blooms in midsummer when most other once-bloomers have completed their cycle of flowers. In my garden, it has exhibited a modest amount of suckering and cane dieback.

In back of this rose, I planted 'Complicata' near a wooden fence covered with turkey wire, stiff wire mesh. So far, this rose has grown 8 feet high and wide and, as its size increases, I coil its long, flexible, almost thornless stems through the stiff metal wires on the fence. The rose's large single blooms—unusual for a Gallica—are rosy pink, with yellow stamens at the center. 'Complicata' has a voluptuous appeal to the senses, quite distinct from many other shrub roses. In this spot, as the rose matures, a sheet of blooms will press against the wooden fence.

One summer, as I was nonchalantly walking and admiring different parts of my garden, I glanced over in the direction of the fence and saw many 2-inch-long, rabbit-foot–like pieces of growth coming off a vine planted near 'Complicata'. I wondered what it was and carefully observed it as it grew over the next week or two. Soon I noticed that the "rabbit's foot" transformed into exquisite drooping purple and white panicles. Suddenly I recalled that almost a decade ago I had planted *Wisteria macrostachya* (Kentucky wisteria). (I've since learned that, especially in northern climates, wisteria often takes seven to ten years to bloom.) I was awestruck by the beauty of the fifteen or so blossoms, and how enchanting they looked next to 'Complicata'. After the wisteria blooms fade, its green, smooth seedpods add an attractive accent.

Other flowers pair well with this pink rose. An excellent pick is *Coreopsis lanceolata* (lanceleaf coreopsis). It has cup-shaped yellow flowers that are 2 inches across; the plant grows to 4 feet and its long, narrow stems easily poke through the roses. I am so pleased with this combination that I let this coreopsis self-sow abundantly in this site. It also scatters itself and looks beautiful near 'Désirée Parmentier'. To keep this coreopsis performing at its peak, I try to remember to deadhead the old blooms so I can have profuse flowers from May into September or until a strong frost zaps the yellow blooms. There are many other varieties of coreopsis and all look attractive when united with the firework exhibition of roses.

In particular, two other short bushy Gallicas, 'Tuscany' and 'Tuscany Superb', are ideal to plant near the sparkly, sunny blooms of any coreopsis. Dating prior to 1500, 'Tuscany' has double blooms that are such a dark red it has been called 'Black Tuscany'. The blooms are set off nicely by its pronounced yellow stamens and the deep green leaves. 'Tuscany Superb' is thought to be a sport of 'Tuscany'. The flowers are similar, but the blooms are fuller and the plant is more vigorous. Since my personality is boisterous, like the rich colors of these Gallicas, they suit my garden style.

Another popular Gallica is 'Cardinal de Richelieu', named after Louis XIII's prime minister. Many are grown in my region: gardeners love its deep purple very double blooms as well as its sweet scent and lack of thorns. This dense 5-foot grower, which continually sends up suckers, can be contained in one spot if new shoots are cut as soon as they appear.

I have an intuitive approach to choosing plants to combine with roses. I push my cart around the nursery and buy whatever I imagine will enhance the beauty of the rose. If it works well, I'm thrilled; if not, I'll move the plants and try something else. I'll also let different annuals and perennials seed themselves in various flower beds. If too many appear for my taste, I simply pull them out.

With these last three boldly colored Gallicas, *Salvia sclarea* and *S. pratensis*, with their pastel shades of lavender, add zip as their flowers poke through the foliage and stems of the roses. Another excellent companion plant is *Lathyrus* spp. (everlasting sweet peas). The white flowers reminiscent of the blooms on pea plants with

hints of pink nicely accent the audacious colors of the Gallica roses, and their tendrils wind easily among the rose stems.

A wonderful Gallica is 'Sissinghurst Castle'. This rose was rediscovered in the late 1940s in Kent, England, on acreage that would eventually become Sissinghurst Castle, the home of Vita Sackville-West, a well-known English gardener and author during the early twentieth century. This compact rose grows under 3 feet and boasts plentiful deep red blooms with golden yellow stamens. Its prickles are red and the foliage is rich green. Place this rose along a path so you and garden visitors can easily take in its aromatic perfume. To accentuate this rose's circular blossom shape and stunning color, I recommend vertical veronicas and salvias in shades of purple and blue as companions. Common snapdragons are favorites of mine, too, with their perky colors of lemony yellow, pink, and red. Years ago, I experimented with the satiny snapdragon 'Black Prince', whose reddish-black flowers would pair nicely with 'Sissinghurst Castle'.

'Cardinal de Richelieu' rose has long-lasting deep purple flowers, which come in small clusters and seem velvety. The whitish center and dark green leaves add a sense of mystery to the picture.

'Alain Blanchard' is a Gallica that is very hardy in the Inter-mountain West region. This dense and bushy shrub, with occasional long arching canes, has slightly semidouble blooms in mottled tones of deep red and purple, which help intensify the distinctive golden stamens. This is one of the "spotted" Gallicas: because of all the characteristic striping, it is often called a "mad" Gallica. This plant is content in a somewhat shaded position, which attests to the fact that Gallicas do well in less than ideal sites—although the colors may be paler and the abundance of flowers may suffer depending on how shaded the area is. 'Alain Blanchard' has been slow to develop at a friend's house, maybe because of its shady location. However, this slow growth can also be a plus, because the rose may sucker less.

There are two more Gallicas that appeal to me. Because of its seductive name, I am tempted to purchase 'La Belle Sultane'. For me, the name conjures up images of slow-moving camels, wavy sandy deserts, and sizzling heat beating down on the land. I visualize powerful women bedecked with turbans and wrapped in fine layers of cloth and silk. The slightly more than five petaled flowers are violet-red. As the fragrant flowers age, their color changes to a softer purple. In the center are pronounced golden stamens. This historical rose, which grew in Empress Josephine's garden at Malmaison, would probably reach 4 feet for gardeners in cold climates.

When in bloom, a Gallica that surpasses most others with its riotous display of blossoms is 'Charles de Mills'. After eight or so years, my shrub has reached 7 feet high by 6 feet wide. Its canes are long: some arch gracefully, while others remain vertical. 'Charles de Mills' is planted in my front garden in a slightly shaded location, but this has not interfered with its flowering. The blossoms have a multitude of petals and sometimes—adding to its beauty—in the center, you'll see a pale green cavity. The flower color varies from dark lilac to crimson-purple to shades of wine—extremely pleasing to the eye. 'Charles de Mills' is nearly thornless and is moderately scented. Like many old garden roses, it suckers freely, yet this has rarely happened thus far.

Blooming around the front edge of 'Charles de Mills' are several coral bells (*Heuchera* spp.). These easy-to-grow perennials with their

ruffled foliage and alluring colored leaves of pewter, plum, and charcoal gray, contrast the medium green leaves of the rose. In a sunny spot near the rose, I grow several *Penstemon* 'Shades of Mango' (beard tongue). In August, when color—aside from daisies, joe-pye weed, and goldenrod—may be flagging in gardens, this penstemon roars with bright, hot colors, such as orange, yellow, and mango.

I conclude this section on Gallicas with 'Belle de Crécy', a rose given to me by a colleague a few years back. The owner complained that, since her soil was sandy, this rose became a nuisance whose shoots were constantly sprouting throughout her garden. (Clay soils, which are dense, will often help discourage rose roots from spreading too aggressively.) Furthermore, her garden space was limited, so it was time to label this plant a pass-along—a familiar tradition many gardeners practice. 'Belle de Crécy', known for its pleasing colors of mauve, gray, and pink, with very quartered flowers, arrived at my doorstep one day early in spring. In exchange, I gave my colleague a piece of *R.* x *alba* 'Semiplena', which flourished in her garden.

Their perfumes, saturated and vibrant colors, and legendary past will always make the Gallica roses special for me.

Left: Rosa x *alba* 'Semiplena' and 'Charles de Mills' rose, with its deep lilac to wine blossoms, are dwarfed in comparison to the robust flower head of giant hogweed (*Heracleum mantegazzianum*).

Right: 'Charles de Mills' rose has many petals and forms a tight globular blossom that appears symmetrical and rather formal.

Damask Roses

Damask roses are closely related to the Gallicas, but mystery surrounds their exact ancestry. The Damask name suggests that these roses may have originated in the region of Damascus in Syria. However, the earliest recorded mention of their existence occurred in sixteenth-century Italy. The once-blooming Damask roses are best known for their distinctive fragrance and are still planted in Bulgaria for the commercial production of rose oil. Many rose historians believe crusaders of the twelfth and thirteenth centuries brought back specimens of this rose from their sojourns to the Middle East, eventually establishing these roses in Europe.

Over the centuries, some Damask roses have disappeared from commerce and there are fewer of them to choose from than from most other classes of old garden roses. Damask roses come in shades of pink and white and are very thorny. However, the thorns become irrelevant when I walk past a blooming bush and breathe in its delicious fragrance and experience its dynamic color.

Even though I have been growing 'Hebe's Lip' for about six years, this Damask has just begun to triumph for me in the past two years. I was drawn to buy 'Hebe's Lip' because of its strange name. Why else would I buy a fragile rose with eight pathetic leaves in a 4-inch black pot? I learned that this rose was named for Hebe, the Greek goddess of youth. I would guess that the word 'lip' may have been added because along the edges of its wavy blush-white semidouble petals are ribbons of red, an unusual characteristic. I'm really glad I've waited for this rose to mature. Currently it is 5 feet high and almost as wide, with green-gray leaves that are scooplike and that remind me of chips to use with a dip for entertaining! I like its odd shape and over-all character—canes seem to grow this way and that in a haphazard fashion. The prickles accompanying its stems are sharp, but not terribly so. On the new growth, some prickles are soft and bend slightly if pushed. Rose lover that I am, I find these maroon-green downward curving prickles attractive, even when the rose is not in bloom. As of yet there has not been any suckering, but each spring I cut off almost 2 feet of dead wood. 'Hebe's Lip' recovers nicely, blooming for a few weeks in midsummer. Scattered here and there like a patch-

A rose with a dainty demureness, 'Hebe's Lip', shows white flowers outlined charmingly, here and there, in pink. The ornamental onion (*Allium caeruleum*) brings in an electrifying shade of blue.

The pure white flowers of 'Madame Hardy' rose complement the rich, green foliage.

work around the rose are a few clumps of a low-growing, lacy white dianthus. It was mislabeled 'Candy Dish' when I bought it: whatever its true name, when I stoop to smell the flower, I inhale a delightful chocolate scent! I also like the vertical lines that 2-foot-tall *Penstemon strictus* (Rocky Mountain penstemon) brings to this area. It looks stunning in summer as its lavender-blue tubular flowers are sprinkled from one end of this bed to the other.

Another Damask that is easy to grow, and one that is significantly better known among rose aficionados, is 'Madame Hardy'. Bred in 1832 by Empress Josephine's head gardener, Monsieur Hardy, this elegant rose is named after his wife. The highly fragrant, exquisitely formed white rose may have one hundred petals and is famous for a splash of green in the center instead of the usual yellow stamens. While some rose experts believe this green dot detracts from the beauty of the rose, I am drawn to the touch of green and love to search it out in each luscious blossom. I do get extensive winterkill on the canes, especially after a bad winter. Yet I easily cut out the dead growth and the 'Madame' comes back strong in June. Her growth habit is upright, slightly vase-shaped, and usually reaches a maximum height of 6 feet. If my garden space were limited and I could only have a few old garden roses, 'Madame Hardy' would be one of the top ones on my list along with 'Alika'.

Among plants that are attractive when 'Madame Hardy' is in bloom are geraniums, coreopsis, and delphiniums. In addition, I am fond of *Campanula medium* (cup-and-saucer). I am attracted to this old-fashioned biennial's large cup-shaped blooms, which come in soft hues of pink and blue.

A very desirable Damask rose that I have seen but have yet to purchase is 'Ispahan'. Its growth habit is strong and vigorous, and its opulent perfume appeals to me, as well as its full and curly blossoms. My own personal name for the double flowers is "Flamingo Pink" because the hot pink color reminds me of the plastic pink flamingo statues that some gardeners use for decoration. Among old garden roses, 'Ispahan' is particularly special because it flowers for almost six weeks, which is long compared to most other once-bloomers, which last only three to four weeks.

I like growing the Damask roses because they add significantly to my collection of old garden roses: their assorted colors and shapes bring diversity and character to my garden. In addition, I find it fascinating that the tradition of making jams, jellies, and perfumes from the Damask rose petals is still alive today as it was thousands of years ago.

The Albas

The Albas are an ancient group of roses that probably existed in medieval times. They are likely descendants of *Rosa canina*. I can visualize their elegant lush growth around castles, moats, and drawbridges. With their tall, graceful forms and heady fragrance, they have an aristocratic air. Yet that nobility does not interfere with their stalwart and rugged constitution. Their thick, thorny, and sturdy canes stand up to a multitude of fierce weather conditions,

'Alba Maxima' rose and the crimson, frilly blooms of 'William Lobb' rose interlace, along with the fine-textured greenery of clematis.

barely exhibiting any dieback—a rose definitely meant for the Rocky Mountain region in which I garden. The flowers of the Albas come in shades of pale pink to creamy white. They are also known for their healthy gray-green foliage and for their minimal suckering.

I grow four Albas, each in a different location and each with unique traits. First, I'll discuss 'Alba Maxima'. Fellow rose lovers, who know how large 'Alba Maxima' can be, are surprised when I say I'm training this rose over an arch. The truth is I am, and it's working. While the canes were young and bendable—an ideal time to begin training—I carefully wove them through the supports of a sturdy black wrought-iron arch. Over several years, these canes have grown to more than 10 feet, and make a dazzling display when the ivory-white double flowers adorn the arbor in June. Scrambling up this rose, peeking through the flowers and greenery, is *Clematis texensis* 'Duchess of Albany'. The vine's pink tubular flowers enhance the picturesque scene. What especially pleases me about this rose is that there has not been much winterkill on the canes. I only need to cut off a few dead sprigs here and there.

Pruning techniques for clematis, like roses, are often perplexing to gardeners. When to cut the plant down is the major question. Many people just ignore their clematis and they do reasonably well. But over time, the plant is likely to become a large tangled mass of twiggy brown growth, or, as Barry Fretwell, author of *Clematis as Companion Plants*, states so well: "All too often, one sees *C. x jackmanii*, or similar, swaying disconsolately in the breeze like a dried corpse on the gallows, its large, tangled mass of 'hair' held high in the air over 8 to 10 feet of lanky brown body". Pruning keeps the plant in bounds and assures continued success of the beautiful fresh flowers. (For pruning tips on clematis, please refer to the bibliography at the end of the book.)

Cooler fall temperatures do not signal the end of the 'Alba Maxima's' performance. Like a live performer going behind the curtain to make a wardrobe change, shiny orange-red rose hips appear on 'Alba Maxima' in fall, shifting the scene. The hips contrast well against the foliage of the rose, along with other flowers that bloom around it in fall, including asters, cosmos, and the silvery leaves of *Artemisia cana* (silver sage).

On the other side of this trellis, I planted *Clematis tibetana*, a very hardy species that is quite perfect for cold climates, since it grows from 6,000 to 15,800 feet in Tibet, northern India, and China. While weeding one year, I accidentally pulled it out and thought I had lost it forever. As good luck would have it, the next year it appeared on the same side as 'Alba Maxima' and bloomed through the foliage. I treasure the blooms of this clematis as much as the flowers on the rose. The four lime-green, wide-open petals on the clematis, which curve back sharply at the tips, are in bloom in September and October and quickly tangle themselves around the greenery of the rose. Until a heavy frost or snow comes along and turns many plants into mush, the silky seed heads of this clematis enhance the rose hips—especially, often in November, when they transform into fuzzy cotton

Left: The floriferous, semidouble blossoms of *Rosa alba* 'Semiplena' braid through the lacy stems and flowers of the colorful cranesbill (*Geranium psilostemon*).

Right: A close-up of *Rosa alba* 'Semiplena' reveals delicate blossoms with yellowish-brown centers.

balls. Don't reject roses that only bloom once, thinking blooms are the end to their pageantry. Broaden your horizons by bringing in other plant material to extend the beauty of these once-bloomers.

Since I learned early on that Albas could tolerate some degree of shade, I planted *R. alba* 'Semiplena' 20 feet or so from my huge, multitrunked cottonwood tree, where it has been content for eight years. This rose is very easy to maintain. The shrub is robust, with brambly canes that arch dramatically, an aspect accentuated because my 'Semiplena' is planted in a raised flower bed. The flowers appear in clusters of pure white with golden centers and are semidouble. In June, it is a star performer with a few supporting characters nearby—the perennials that add drama to the scene.

This area receives morning sun, which has satisfied the stately *Eremurus* spp. (foxtail lily) planted near 'Semiplena'. I like the Eiffel Tower–like shape of *Eremurus*, as well as its wide range of pastel colors, including pink-orange, pale yellow, and even a clear white. They bloom in a quirky fashion, from the bottom up, and remain in flower, like the rose, for a few weeks. After the colors of the foxtail lily have faded, the dark green, pea-sized seedpods are attractive. *Sidalcea candida* (prairie mallow) is also near this rose. Related to the common

hollyhock but smaller in size, its white flowers, touched faintly in the center with pink, bloom in dense spikes.

In early fall, after the perennials have finished blooming, hips appear on *R. alba* 'Semiplena'. In shape, size, and color they are almost identical to the hips of 'Alba Maxima', probably because these two roses are close cousins. Beneath the shiny and abundant hips is a large swath of *Ceratostigma plumbaginoides* (leadwort). The shiny red hips of the 'Semiplena', together with the blue flowers and the maroon foliage of the leadwort, embellish the fall garden.

My earliest Alba acquisition was 'Pompon Blanc Parfait'. The name appealed to me—it sounded delicate and cute—and the tight, double blooms truly look like white powder puffs, tinged slightly pink, smaller and different from those of most other Albas. It also has a delightful light scent. The canes are not overly thorny—but will give a few pricks to bare flesh. Its growth habit is erect, with a slight outward bend near the top. Mine has reached 5

Around Thanksgiving, the orange and red hips of *Rosa alba* 'Semiplena' trail over a weathered wooden fence.

In June, the white rose 'Pompon Blanc Parfait' squeezes between the palmlike foliage of joe-pye weed (*Eupatorium purpureum maculatum* 'Gateway') and the bending leaves of ornamental grass (*Miscanthus sinensis* 'Variegatus').

feet high and 4 feet wide. 'Pompon Blanc Parfait' blooms longer than most other Albas, usually from mid-June into mid-July.

This rose took at least six years to mature fully. Most years I experience a great deal of winterkill on the canes, requiring that I cut it down to almost 2 feet or less in early spring. But it still gathers enough momentum to burst forth with inviting blooms by midsummer.

At the base of this rose and blooming at the same time, I have planted *Geranium* 'Patricia', known for its showy magenta-pink flowers, highlighted with a dark center. This hardy geranium has wiry-thin 3-foot stems that wiggle into the rose foliage. Even in early fall when the rose has long-since completed its blooming, the geranium is still luminous and blends well with the gray-green leaves of the rose. As much as I take pleasure in interplanting these roses with perennials, I also like the easy care and visual appeal of certain shrubs with the roses. One with distinctive characteristics is *Salix integra* 'Hakuro Nishiki', a willow planted close to 'Pompon Blanc Parfait'. The willow's multicolored cream, pink, and green leaves are bold and bright in spring; in fall, the foliage is cream-colored and green.

The final Alba I grow is 'Maiden's Blush'. Strong, thorn-proof gloves are definitely in order when pruning this rose or weeding around it. The canes are stiff, with most shooting straight up to 5 feet high, and a few going off diagonally. The cleanly cupped, deep pink flowers, which fade to white, are drenched with a strong perfume. The amount of dieback on the canes is irregular, some years a few inches and other times a foot or two. A good companion plant, which makes dense mats around this rose, is *Geranium macrorrhizum*, with its clusters of pale lavender flowers. This drought-tolerant geranium is known for its scented leaves, which are highly potent when gently rubbed between the fingers.

The Albas are my favorites of all the old garden roses, in particular because of their elegant demeanor and the husky rose hips many of them produce. To know that, in my humble half-acre garden, I'm growing plants that are descendants of roses that grew in medieval times definitely excites me!

Centifolias

Centifolias are also known as cabbage roses because of their abundant petals, which overlap like leaves on a cabbage, hiding the center of the rose. Some historians believe Centifolias existed as early as 400 B.C., but the general consensus is that they evolved in Holland during the sixteenth century. The flowers are globular and appear in clusters once a year in summer. Some are slightly dense, while others have an open, branching habit. A distinguishing trait is their slightly crinkled foliage. Color ranges from white through deep rose, and they are fragrant.

I have just one *Centifolia*, 'Rose de Meaux', which is newly planted. Although it is the only one in my garden, I have discovered some intriguing facts. Miss Ellen Willmott, an expert rosarian, (1860–1934) said it seemed probable that this rose may have come from the garden of Domenique Seguier, Bishop of Meaux (1637), who was a great rose connoisseur for his time.

I anxiously await its tidy pink pompon-shaped blossoms, which some authors say resemble the flowers of a dianthus. This is a miniature variety. Since I doubt it will get above 15 inches, I have placed it toward the front of a shrub border. Low-growing shrubs like this one are excellent used en masse at the edge of any perennial or shrub border where their flowers can be prominently displayed.

These classic old garden roses were quite popular in Dutch gardens and therefore with Dutch old masters who used them in paintings in the sixteenth and seventeenth centuries. I will buy more Centifolias to add to the diversity of my rose collection. One that I may purchase, particularly because it is known to perform well in cold climates, is 'Village Maid'. Under 4 feet, it has soft off-white double blooms generously splashed with pink. It is floriferous when the flower appears in late June and even offers some repeat-blooming in late summer.

Moss Roses

Moss roses, fashionable during the Victorian era, developed as sports of Centifolias. The stems of most Moss roses are heavily clothed with a mosslike growth that sets these roses apart from other old garden roses. The buds, too, are covered with this mossy growth, which is mildly sticky and fragrant, yet most are soft to touch. Some gardeners unfamiliar with Moss roses at first think this growth is a disease or fungus, rather than a natural part of the rose.

'William Lobb' is a Moss rose planted next to my 'Alba Maxima' rose. The long, rigid (yet somewhat bendable when young) green stems, covered with sharp bristles, have reached about 7 feet. I have trained a few of these stems to climb through a metal arbor. Overall, when this rose is trained in this manner, it appears gangly and awkward. But the silky, mauve-purple fragrant flowers, which appear once the unusually attractive, pointy green buds open, make up for any structural shortcomings. In fall, I like to touch and admire this rose's round orange hips, which are also coated in this highly textured mossy growth. In summer and fall, after the pink *Clematis texensis* 'Duchess of Albany' has finished blooming, its coppery, filigreed seed heads are peppered throughout this rose. The shape of the seed heads reminds me of a child's fast-spinning pinwheel toy. I'm not much for decoration in the garden, other than the plants themselves, but here I have hung a few glasslike, half-dollar–sized reflective ornaments. They gently hang down from a thin wire around the rose blossoms, adding sparkle and reflection to all the surrounding plants. As I write in my office, it's a pleasure to glance out my window and see the silhouette of these mirrors dancing about my patch of grass.

I thought I had 'Salet', another Moss rose, in my garden. However, upon closer inspection, my reddish puffy rose didn't have enough moss to qualify as a Moss rose. A fellow rose expert also told me my rose was mislabeled. (Mail-order nurseries and local garden centers sometimes make mistakes or labels get lost.) We were both unsure as to the exact identity of the rose I had, although I believe it is an old garden rose, since it only blooms for a few weeks in June.

One day I hope to purchase the real 'Salet', which would be perfect, at 3 feet high and wide, for one of my small flower beds. The double flowers are bright pink, sweetly scented, and have a loose appearance. What is special about 'Salet' is that it is repeat-blooming.

A Moss rose that has become rather mature for me in recent years is 'Goethe'. A vigorous bush, it grows more than 5 feet high and 4 feet wide. It is very prickly and the buds have a great deal of brownish moss on them. Sometimes I like to squeeze the buds between my fingers to savor their stickiness and fully appreciate the mossy texture, as well as to feel the plumpness of the bud. The prickles are burgundy colored and play off well against the dark green leaves that are etched sparingly in red. The well-cupped, magenta-pink flowers have a yellow center and bloom one time in early summer. 'Goethe' handles Colorado's tough winters rather well, with little damage to its stout canes.

My rose guru, Graham Stuart Thomas, gave a rave review to the Moss rose 'Général Kléber'. He praised its "clear and refined

The 'Goethe' rose exhibits noteworthy crimson to pink blossoms, set off by white and yellow centers.

beauty," the double blooms, which are large, cotton-candy pink, and fragrant. I saw this elegant, bushy rose at a local display garden only five miles from my house. It's been growing there for a number of years, which means it is likely to be a good performer in my area. At 4 feet high and wide, it's another nice choice for a small garden. It is heavily mossed on the stems and buds, a feature that appeals to me. There are a few inches of dieback on the canes, but not a cumbersome amount.

If I ever plant this rose in my garden, I will place *Nectaroscordum siculum* (Sicilian onion) around it. I have used this onion-related bulb near other low-growing roses where the long, thin stems jut through the rose foliage. At 3 to 4 feet high, from a central axis, twenty or more graceful bells dangle down a few inches. Each bellflower is greenish white, accented with strong tints of rose-purple. Once the flowers have finished blooming, the vertical stalk and the hanging bells turn the color of hay, which presents a stark accent

among the lush greenery of roses and nearby perennials. Another excellent perennial to intersperse with roses is *Iris pallida* 'Variegata'. I have many throughout my garden. Their thick green and creamy-yellow striped leaves, which have a gentle point at the tip, plus their heady purple flowers, add diversity to the rose scene.

A rare find for me several years ago was the Moss rose 'Lanei' or sometimes spelled 'Laneii'. Many books, mostly those written in warmer climates or where there is considerably more moisture, speak of this rose reaching 6 feet tall. I'm doubtful mine will grow that tall; more likely in my windy backyard, with very few trees for

Blossoms of the pink 'Maiden's Blush' rose intertwine with *Allium caeruleum*.

In bud, 'Lanei' rose shows its distinctive mossy texture. The wavy blossom with many petals is highly appealing as well. (Photo by Marlea A. Graham)

protection, this rose will remain compact and under 4 feet. Heavily mossed on the stems and buds, the rose's dark green, coarse leaves, with serrated edges, encircle clusters of deep pink flowers that carry a rich perfume. This is a tough rose that will tolerate poor soils. To contrast the texture of the rose's leaf and to add an uncommon perennial to your garden, try the 3-foot-tall *Crambe maritima* (sea kale). The sea kale has blue-green smooth foliage that is very wavy, topped by delicate white flowers.

I am on a quest for more Moss roses. I dream of planting various ones at eye level around the edges of my flower beds, so all who visit could recognize and touch the unequaled textured foliage of these antique roses.

CHAPTER THREE

Roving Ramblers and Climbers

Rambling and climbing roses are charming, elegant, and often breathtaking. They conjure up romantic images of English castles, weddings, and paradise as they trail, climb, and spill over fences, walls, houses, and trellises. Their carefree and lax nature makes them useful and appealing to a wide audience. Once simple techniques are grasped, climbers and ramblers can be molded, moved, and tied up and around practically any sturdy structure. They can also trail over hills, banks, and rock walls. Of the more than fifty categories of roses—including hybrid teas, floribundas, miniatures, and Polyanthas—climbers may be best equipped to cast a spell over many gardeners, myself included. Avid gardeners want these precious roses to crawl over their balconies and soar up

'New Dawn' rose trailing atop a fence, is accented by an unknown red rose, plus the bold foliage of plume poppy (*Macleyea cordata*) and the variegated leaves of ribbon grass (*Pharlaris arundinacea* 'Picta').

their front porches, showing their voluptuous faces and dispersing their perfume into the warm evening air.

There is a technical distinction between climbers and ramblers. Climbers are basically large shrubs, many quite vigorous, with mostly stiff long canes off of which smaller blooming branches grow. Ramblers, on the other hand, usually have thinner, more pliable canes that hug the earth and many of them easily root into the ground wherever they touch. This chapter discusses both kinds of roses.

My definition of a climbing rose is *very* broad. Some roses may not officially be defined as climbers or ramblers, but given some form of nearby support, many shrub roses will climb on their own initiative into trees or over fences and arbors. The extent of their growth in colder regions of the country varies widely. Because many shrub roses have long or medium-sized arching canes, they can be deliberately trained to behave like climbers: for this reason, I place them in the category of short climbers. Other roses do not arch very high, but can still climb somewhat and be trained and wound over and through a structure.

To cultivate climbing roses successfully, a few details need to be addressed. First, choose climbers that are reliably cold hardy in your area. How do you know what is hardy and works in your region? Talk with gardeners who have firsthand knowledge (i.e., hands-on experience) with growing these roses. Ask yourself how much attention you want to give your rose. Do you want to mulch every year? Do you want to tie them down with twine and burlap, which will make for a winter garden project around Thanksgiving? How much cane dieback is there and how quickly does the rose recover, if at all? Remember, because climbers have additional height, more of the plant is exposed to winter cane injury than in shorter sister roses.

Sometimes, a gardener will just fall in love with a rose's bloom. For instance, 'Gloire de Dijon', popular because of its deep buff-yellow double flowers, is a climber that in England, Oregon, or parts of the East Coast grows 10 to 15 feet. In the Intermountain West, this same rose may not reach those heights unless it's planted in a protected spot, is carefully mulched, or winters are mild. 'Gloire de Dijon' is also prone to diseases, so I would stay away from this variety, since there are a host of equally beautiful climbers, which will withstand fickle weather patterns and bloom more dependably each season without all the fuss. Each gardener needs to decide how much time and energy he or she wants to give a particular rose choice.

Another undeniable fact about climbing roses is that generally they do not, by themselves, latch on or twine up structures like a clematis does. They need human hands to guide and gently train them; otherwise, they can become a cobwebby tangle of canes, which looks awkward and unkempt. This appearance is definitely acceptable if for a particular shrub, in a particular setting, you desire that look. Another option is to train a portion of the rose vertically, while other canes are left to scramble about on the ground, surrounded by other plants. In some situations you may want to obscure a structure totally (maybe you have a chain-link fence or an ugly shed that you want to hide). The choice is yours. Here I divide favorite climbers and ramblers by color, and I discuss how I handle different ones, each in its own setting.

Tickle Me Pink

For about four years, I have been growing the Japanese climbing miniature rose 'Nozomi'. This rose has tiny pinkish-white buds, which open up into mostly very pale pink, almost white, single, lightly scented flowers. 'Nozomi' puts on a grand show for a few weeks in June. Flowers trail gracefully along its long, thorny stems, which have reached 4 feet in length. 'Nozomi' is nestled against my house and meanders over a pocket-sized rock garden. In this setting, it does receive some protection from strong winds and other winter hazards. Because of rugged climatic conditions in the Rockies, I don't expect that this rose will grow huge; but I am very satisfied with the fountain of blooms it produces each summer. In spite of its rather short stature, I am attracted to its delicate foliage and pointed shiny green leaves, which are traced with red in the fall. As I was examining its fall coloration, I came upon a few polished dark red rose hips about the size of a pinhead, which adds a special element to this rose.

Overflowing with many bunches of nodding clusters of dark red rose hips in early fall is *Rosa eglanteria* (sweet briar), a species

'Nozomi' rose has wide-spreading, pearly pink petals, accented by a yellow center.

rose that stands out against my sky-blue house. In spring, this once-blooming ancient rose is not shy about producing soft pink single flowers. The flower is sweetly scented. But this rose is famous for the apple perfume that it exudes, especially in spring, when the leaves are rubbed between one's fingers—suddenly, a pitcher of apple cider seems to be resting on the nearby picnic table. On a historical note, in Colonial days this rose was used as a hedge plant. Regular shearing promoted new growth. Because of drier conditions, colder temperatures, and lack of consistent and sufficient snow cover, shearing this rose low to the ground is not recommended in cold regions of the country. In fact, it is likely that this rose would require a number of years to rejuvenate itself were it sheared thusly.

R. eglanteria is a good example of a rose that would make an excellent climber, if trained as such. However, it also displays its leaves and flowers very well when some of its lax canes tumble over a nearby rock garden. As Thanksgiving approaches, some

Purple meadow sage (*Salvia nemorosa*) pokes through the single blossoms of *Rosa eglanteria*, commonly known as the sweet briar rose.

leaves from my *R. eglanteria* have fallen, while a few are still green, and others are yellow, etched in red, and holding fast to the thorny canes. In late fall and winter, the shrub drips with bunches of seemingly lacquered red fruits on slightly brick-colored canes. When spring turns the corner, *Muscari armeniacum* 'Blue Spike' (grape hyacinth), fuller than the wild form, can be seen blooming with its flax blue flowers beneath the masses of colorful rose hips. One year, for a different look in spring and summer, I did a mass planting of *Portulaca grandiflora* (moss rose). Among many color choices, such as yellow, orange, and salmon, I chose double cherry red. This low-growing, drought-tolerant succulent annual was a perfect match to *R. eglanteria*, which also likes hot dry locations.

R. eglanteria is well fortified with thorns. I try to remember to wear long pants and strong gloves when I prune this favorite rose, but I often forget and just grab my tools on the spur of the moment. Many times I come away from pruning with scratches and bloody legs and arms. This is a scenario to which many rose

Top left: In October, all the hips on *Rosa eglanteria* turn a vibrant red-orange.

Top right: As fall progresses, leaves on *R. eglanteria* turn yellowish, creating a potent contrast to the rose hips.

Right: Often the hips of *R. eglanteria* stay on the shrub through winter and make a pretty companion next to spring-blooming grape hyacinth (*Muscari armeniacum* 'Blue Spike').

growers can relate. If minor pain and the sight of blood send you into a panic, you can bundle up, covering all limbs before you prune. You can also let the rose go wild forever. Or you can choose a rose that is not so large and vigorous. Each gardener needs to find his or her own solution. My own answer is to deal with a few cuts and scratches. I'm also pleased that since, after eight years, this rose has not suckered, I need prune for only a few hours.

Every two or three years, depending on my mood, the weather, and the needs of this rose, I enter the briar patch once most of the leaves have fallen and do some serious thinning, cutting out aged, brown, and thick canes. This enables the rose to produce new healthy growth. I also look for any dead wood or weak and spindly growth and carefully remove it, pruning old canes to the ground. By observing the canes closely, I can easily distinguish the old, worn-out canes from the new growth. The new growth is thinner, greener with tints of burgundy, and has a more lively appearance overall.

A rose that has been a companion of mine for many years is 'Banshee'. Experts differ as to how to categorize this rose, some placing it with the Gallicas, others with the Damasks. I'll leave the bickering to the botanists and rosarians as I blissfully enjoy its lush perfume and robust blooms that appear for a few weeks in June. Located on the south side, near the end of my property, this rose stands out as I walk to my backyard garden. Its 8-foot-long, thick, thorny canes, which bend near the top, poke through *Cytisus* x *praecox* (Warminster broom), which has yellow pealike flowers on pencil-thin evergreen stems and is planted only a few feet away. The broom and rose bloom simultaneously for a few days in June, looking like perfect partners intertwined with each other. Once fall approaches, 'Banshee' displays a rich tapestry of fall foliage colors, including mahogany, tawny brown, and yellow. These colors look even more exuberant when they grow in between the decorative sprigs of the evergreen broom, enhancing the winter landscape.

'Banshee', like many roses with varied growth habits, can serve a wide range of purposes in the modern landscape. Although not considered a climber, 'Banshee' can definitely be used in this fashion.

The full-petaled blossoms of 'Banshee' rose echo the pinkish-purple flowers of *Malva sylvestris* 'Zebrina'.

Years ago, in an old Denver neighborhood, I admired how a home-owner had gently trained it to amble over a white fence. In a well-established Boulder, Colorado, neighborhood, colleagues have told me that this rose has scrambled up a tree where it reaches more than 8 feet high.

The needs of this rose are minimal. From time to time, I have crawled beneath it to thin out some of the canes: there is little winter damage. A few suckers appear now and then, but I eliminate them with ease. Regarding irrigation, my neighbor keeps his grass manicured and carefully watered. Some of this water flows to the base of my rose, so I've never had to give it any additional water. Even without his runoff water, I believe this rose is drought-tolerant once established.

Another rose that I rarely water is 'Hiawatha Recurrent'. Some of this is due to location, since it receives some runoff from a nearby flower bed. In addition, it is located in the third of my backyard

The profuse blossoms of 'Banshee' rose gently trail over a white gate.

garden that is in a large pocket, which holds moisture longer and dries out later in summer than other spots. I happened upon 'Hiawatha Recurrent' a number of years ago. While visiting a friend's summer garden, I admired the plant's long pencil-like canes and practically drooled over its lipstick red single blooms, dabbed with white toward the center and a dot of yellow in the very middle. The many clusters of flowers almost smothered the diminutive, shiny green leaves. "Would you like a cutting?" she asked quite calmly. As one gardener to another, I'm sure she noticed my eagerness. "Of course, of course," I sputtered.

I sped home and quickly planted this rambling rose. I tucked it in along a low granite wall, where it effortlessly took hold. It has become quite content in this spot. The long, spraying stems crawl through the nooks and crannies of my wall and also swirl onto my gravel path. Because of its aggressive nature, it even scurries 6 feet up *Viburnum lentago* (nannyberry), a small tree planted nearby.

'Hiawatha Recurrent' rose twists among granite stone as floppy iris leaves bend off to one side.

'Hiawatha Recurrent's' only drawback is that it is scentless. But this rose more than makes up for this modest deficiency. It blooms later than many other roses, from the end of June far into mid-July. For the first two or three years after I planted 'Hiawatha Recurrent', the repeat-bloom was excellent, but now, I just get a smattering of blossoms that come in September and October. However, I do enjoy the pin-sized bunches of dark red hips that are randomly scattered on the ends of the branches, where summer blossoms appeared. Although difficult to find, there are mail-order sources that carry it if you can't find this variety at your local nursery.

The brilliance of this rose is magnified when it is accompanied by a few choice perennials. In my garden, *Euphorbia seguieriana* (Seguier's spurge), a foot-tall graceful plant with lime-yellow bracts, is nearby; also close are irises, with smooth, linear foliage. The euphorbia produces reddish foliage in the fall and glimmers in the sunlight. In addition to these two perennials, *Sphaeralcea munroana* (Munro's globe

mallow) has happily seeded itself in this bed, shooting like an arrow straight up through the rose foliage to show off its saucer-shaped orange flowers. The scene is completed by the many cobwebby *Sempervivum* (hen and chickens) that I have shoved into this rickety wall over the years.

Hen and chickens are a story unto themselves. Years ago, I started with half a dozen plants. Now thousands grace much of my landscape, scrambling around small plants, walls, rock gardens, troughs, and paths. I have found that some of these *Sempervivum* produce attractive flowers, while others do not. Their knitted foliage patterns, colors, and compact forms are diverse and their childlike size is appealing. Propagation is easy: simply detach offsets when they are well grown and press them into the ground—almost any time of year works. When I teach, I bring handfuls of these along, passing them out to students. Beginners grab them up, realizing they multiply fast, shun any care, and require almost

'Hiawatha Recurrent' rose mingles in summer with the chartreuse florets of spurge (*Euphorbia seguieriana*).

The flowers of 'May Queen' rose nestle among medium-green leaves.

no moisture. Just give them sharply drained, slightly gravelly soil and a sunny site.

I have planted a basket-shaped trough, overflowing with hen and chicks, near 'May Queen', a rambler that I'm hoping to train as a climber. I purchased it at a rose symposium. While fellow rose enthusiasts dashed around trying to make the best purchase, I was checking with colleagues as to its hardiness and potential success in my rugged, cold, and often snowless winters. The tag noted that it had *Rosa wichurana* lineage, which signaled the strong likelihood of its hardiness. However, it will probably not be as "spirited" as it might be on the East or West Coasts. It will likely reach 8 or 10 feet in height, as compared with 15 feet or more in warmer climates.

The foliage on 'May Queen' is similar, but larger, than that of *R. wichurana*. Its thorns look a bit menacing, yet appealing because of their deep red-blood color on young plants, which is dramatic against the immature lime-green stems. Overall, thorns go with roses. We don't necessarily want the thorns, but we don't have much of a choice if we want to grow these beautiful creatures. I often recall Graham Stuart Thomas's comments on thorns and roses. He philosophizes that the thorns accentuate the beauty of the rose and that this juxtaposition of opposites parallels life, with the constant and flowing balance between good and evil.

In spite of the thorns of 'May Queen', I thoroughly enjoy its light scent and coral-pink flowers. They are small, rather flat, and evoke memories of a pink mint candy I used to let melt in my mouth as a child. Training this rose to climb at this stage of its development, after four years, is ideal; I have two pliable stems twined around a pillar on my patio. As these main canes increase vertically, I will gently bend and guide them horizontally around my structure, remembering that these roses bloom more fruitfully from side shoots, which come off the main canes, than they do from canes growing straight up. However you grow 'May Queen', I suggest pairing it with *Phuopsis stylosa* (crosswort). I have been growing this uncommon, sprawling ground cover for almost a decade. The purplish-pink, 1½-inch clusters of flowers on this plant resemble a pincushion. This ground cover has an odd scent that appeals to some, while others find it unpleasant and have suggested it smells like a skunk. Even when the flowers are finished, I like the mat-forming, dense, sea-green mound it makes. In this area of my garden, I have planted the bulb *Allium karataviense* 'Ivory Queen'. It reaches about 6 inches high, topped off by a pale lime-green umbel about the size of a baseball. The width and smooth texture of the greenish leaves is striking against the smaller deep green leaves of the rose.

An all-time favorite double pink climber that has been a staple for more than sixty years is 'New Dawn'. It has won awards for beauty and is ideal for gardeners in tough climates. There is very little winter dieback on the canes; it's fast growing, quite fragrant, and heartily repeat-blooms into fall. Canes will reach about 10 feet and its dark green leaves are somewhat glossy. It would look excellent draping over a short wall, or woven through a low chain-link fence to create a beautiful barrier or hedge. Wherever you

Award-winning climbing rose 'New Dawn' is tough and hardy in cold parts of this country and continually churns out a profusion of flowers from June until first frost.

display it, make sure 'New Dawn' can be seen by passersby, who, in fall, might enjoy seeing a few rose hips.

An excellent perennial to combine with 'New Dawn' is *Macleaya cordata* (plume poppy). This grandiose plant needs room, since it often reaches 6 feet in height, even for northern gardeners. The leaves, with their intricate shape, olive-green color, and off-white backs, are captivating. I'm also fond of the rosy-colored, fluffy plumes, which are soft to touch. When I breeze by, I enjoy gathering a bundle in my hands. These features combine well with the dark green foliage of 'New Dawn'. Some gardeners consider *M. cordata* too "friendly" for their garden, meaning it is invasive. However, in certain situations, especially if there is some shade and moisture is kept at bay, its aggressive behavior can be curtailed.

Another pink climber is 'Jeanne LaJoie'. The surprise with this rose is that it is a miniature climber. The blooms are small. About 2

Miniature climbing rose 'Jeanne LaJoie' produces fluffy, pink double blossoms that are lightly scented.

inches across, they appear in bunches and carry a light fragrance. This rose in bloom reminds one of mounds of pink cotton candy and it blooms throughout the season. Don't let the term "miniature" fool you—it refers to the bloom and leaf size, not the size and shape of the overall shrub. This rose is quite vigorous. A colleague of mine has grown it for more than a decade; it is more than 8 feet high and just as wide! Another friend grows this rose and has kept it low, to 4 feet, creating a hedge out of many plants. It's fun to be creative with roses. My own specimen has been in for four years, so it is just getting started. I'm training the 6-foot canes—which experience minimal dieback over winter—to spiral up a circular metal trellis where 'Jeanne LaJoie' will command attention, surrounded by ornamental grasses and many daisylike flowers. In midsummer, some of the flowers of 'Jeanne LaJoie' seem to sparkle as they poke through the stems of the spring-blooming shrub *Lonicera syringantha* var. *wolfii* (lilac-flowering dwarf honeysuckle), which, at that time of year and into the fall, has a smattering of orange-red berries.

'Baltimore Belle' rose is a vigorous grower, with hundreds of white flowers. Here it scrambles up a metal structure alongside the trunk of a large tree. (Photo courtesy of Al Ford)

Much larger and even more energetic than 'Jeanne LaJoie' is the reliable and winter-hardy 'Baltimore Belle'. A colleague planted this boisterous grower alongside a cast-iron arch near a window so that her daughter, whose bedroom was nearby, could enjoy its abundant mass of color and inhale its light fragrance. After ten years it spreads more than 6 feet wide and 15 feet high. Its blooming cycle begins with reddish buds, which open to blush-pink, fully double flowers that fade to white. The blooms of 'Baltimore Belle' appear in clusters that droop and remain showy on the bush from July into August. Once winter has plowed through the landscape and spring approaches, old canes and dead wood should be removed from this rose. This winter/spring pruning allows more sunlight and air to seep into the center of the plant, stimulating new growth and flowers.

The clematis 'Niobe', with robust reddish-purple flowers, is planted a few feet from 'Baltimore Belle'. This easily grown clematis cultivar consistently repeat-blooms over a long season. The spidery tendrils of the clematis grasp the rose canes and its healthy mid-green foliage.

Clouds of pink roses, many that perfume the air, are ideal companions as they dart in and out among the shades of green plants and a rainbow of gorgeous perennials. They mesh especially well with silver foliage plants, such as *Artemisia* 'Powis Castle' and *A. cana* (silver sage), which highlight the resonant colors of both plants.

Although not a pink at all (in fact the blossoms are colored deep red), the climbing rose 'Dortmund' is a favorite. I've grown this rose for a decade, moving it several times until it is finally content where it is planted. Wavy petals, numbering about seven, accented with a white eye, are one of its distinctive traits, along with

'Dortmund' rose blooms prolifically around a curly arbor and is complemented by the rich yellow flowers of a columbine.

glossy, deep green foliage, an unusual characteristic in shrub roses. In climates with more rainfall, it may climb more than 10 feet, but around the "Mile High City"—and I'm half an hour away from Denver—it reaches about 8 feet tall. I wind its long, stout, and thorny canes through a sturdy metal arbor. Sometimes there are ten blossoms on a stem, and the grape-sized, bright red fruits that appear afterward dangle in big clusters like decorations on a Christmas tree! After it rests now and then in the heat of the summer, it repeat-blooms. Although there is dieback on the cane after most winters, this is minimal and easy to attend.

Since I've planted many climbers recently, experience has taught me some valuable lessons. At first, I thought it would be smart to plant these shrubs a foot or so away from where I wanted them to climb, thinking that I would easily pull the canes over and twine them up the structure. But not all climbers have canes that can be readily manipulated. Some are more flexible than others. While this approach will be successful in the long run, next time I plant climbers I'm going to place them only a few inches from the structure. This way they can start to climb sooner. Ten or twenty years down the road, it won't matter at all where they were initially planted. Use whatever method works best for you.

Cottontail White

'Bobbie James' is a once-blooming rampant climber that has taken off like a weed in a friend's garden. Her planting site is somewhat protected by enormous trees and a large old greenhouse. In the first year, this rose grew a remarkable 7 feet up and 8 feet across. This is a happy plant! Eventually it halted its growth at 30 feet. The stems are strong and armed with sharp hooks. Even in this partially shaded site, it is smothered with bending bunches of small semidouble white flowers, dabbed yellow in the center. These are generously scented and bloom for a few weeks in summertime. 'Bobbie James' often comes through the winter quite unscathed, rarely having much dieback on the canes, which turn maroon in cold weather. Groups of spherical orange hips drape 'Bobbie

James' in fall and winter. At the base of this rose, try a recent intro-duction such as *Coreopsis* 'Limerock Ruby' to continue the succes-sion of flowers. It has purple-red, daisylike flowers that grow to about 12 inches high on thin emerald-green foliage. When planted in fairly sunny positions, it blooms incessantly from summer into fall. For the historically curious, 'Bobbie James' is a modern rose in-troduced in 1960, named after an avid gardening friend of Graham Stuart Thomas.

'Darlow's Enigma' is a fantastic rose of unknown parentage, originally discovered by chance in a Eugene, Oregon, garden by Michael Darlow; hence the name. Climbing white roses that repeat-bloom are rarities in the rose kingdom, making this rose's willingness to climb a special treat. 'Darlow's Enigma' offers a light, sweet fragrance and is tolerant of some shade. In addition, it is hardy to minus 20 degrees and likely to survive minus 30 degrees

The dainty flowers of 'Darlow's Enigma' rose are a delightful companion to the yellowish leaves and purple flowers of spiderwort (*Tradescantia* 'Sweet Kate').

in a protected spot, away from low cold pockets or powerful desiccating winds. The blooms are like snow-white saucers from a fine porcelain tea set, offset by lemon-yellow centers, and the reddish-green canes have few thorns. Its growth habit is upright and not as rampant as some other climbers. It even produces a scant quantity of small red rose hips come fall. There is very little winterkill on the canes, and the disease-resistant foliage is dark green and glossy. 'Darlow's Enigma' has been grown successfully for at least ten years in the Denver area, which attests to its hardiness and longevity in the fluctuating conditions of the Intermountain West. My specimen is only two years old, but a gardener in my neighborhood has grown it for many years and trained it over a sturdy wooden arbor. Eventually 'Darlow's Enigma' will max out at about 10 feet high, with a spread of 6 feet.

As mentioned earlier, clematis plants are exceptional companions to grow in and around roses. They help fill in gaps along the rose canes where there are no flowers. Because of its pure white blooms, 'Darlow's Enigma' easily mixes with any number of colorful clematis, such as the summer-blooming *C.* x *aromatica*, known for its small, star-shaped, deep purple flowers with creamy white centers and lemony scent. The familiar *C.* x *jackmanii*, with its large purple face, would look wonderful weaving through the rose canes. Finally, I encourage gardeners to try *C.* 'Proteus, with a pinkish-lavender flower'. Typical of most clematis, *C.* 'Proteus' takes a few years to mature. In recent years, it has come through triumphantly in my garden, towering above grasses and other perennials. This summer-blooming, blowsy clematis has enormous flowers similar to those of a peony. Since I am so enamored with this variety, I plan on buying another *C.* 'Proteus' so it can cling to the canes of 'Darlow's Enigma' and harmonize with the white flowers.

White roses generate purity in gardens. Having no color per se, they mix well with a host of other landscape materials. I like to see their flowers pierce through tons of perennials, bringing more life to all the plants.

Sunshine Yellows

Yellow is often a predominant color in gardens, whether from forsythia, Scotch broom, daisies, or remarkable roses. The climbers are no exception. 'Lawrence Johnston', a beautiful yellow rose, has gained in popularity across the country, especially in recent years and for gardeners in harsh climates. Colorado gardeners have grown it for at least twenty years; even after only six years at a local public garden, the robust canes are more than 2 inches in diameter. Upon maturity, canes can reach 15 feet, possibly more, with minimal dieback after winter. The fact that this highly respected rose performs so well in difficult climatic conditions, tremendously increases its value.

This rose's warm yellow semidouble blooms, with large petals, appear relaxed and floppy, folding over each other as they bloom furiously in June. The blooms sometimes repeat intermittently in summer and fall. In addition, 'Lawrence Johnston' carries a scent—I don't recall the power of its fragrance, although different garden authors, in terms of scent have given it mixed reviews. Some say it's great, while others detest the scent—it's all very subjective. My plant is young, but I anticipate a spectacular display as it winds its way through my sturdy wooden trellis. I look forward to masses of yellow flowers against the blue background of my house.

Recently, I discovered that I have two 'Lawrence Johnston' roses. I thought my other yellow rose was 'Goldbusch', but a colleague told me I was mistaken. (I'm glad I have colleagues and friends who assist me with rose identification.) I had wondered about this rose, since it seemed bigger than I thought 'Goldbusch' should be. With my second 'Lawrence Johnston', I have let the pastel peachy flowers of *Papaver triniifolium* generously flower throughout this area. They meld perfectly with the rose, blooming on and off through the summer, taking breaks when the heat sizzles more than they can stand.

There are other yellow-blended flowers and apricot-shaded climbers to try. For instance I'm growing the 'Alchemist', which I initially bought because of my interest in alchemy. Dating from the

Above: The yellow, mostly single flowers of 'Lawrence Johnston' rose wind up a white gazebo.

Right: After just a few years, 'Lawrence Johnston' rose, with its light and dark yellow blossoms, has climbed up a circular metal support.

Middle Ages, alchemy dealt with the transformation, mostly metaphorical, of lead into gold. The 'Alchemist' has been growing in my garden for five years and is more than 8 feet tall, probably close to its maximum size. Although the vigorous, spiny canes are generally upright, when they were young, thinner, and much more manageable, I guided them around my metal arbor (now they look like curly noodles). Only 3 feet wide at present, this shrub will increase in width to about 6 feet. Already, many side shoots spring forth from the two main canes. This once-blooming rose is extremely fragrant, with very double blossoms in a luscious shade of apricot, reminding me of the moist and tender dried apricots I snack on. The foliage is rich green and somewhat bronzy. Not known to be extremely hardy in cold climates, I would mulch this rose well over winter in cold climates.

The linear lines of meadow sage (*Salvia nemorosa*) bend near the peachy pink blossoms and buds of 'Alchemist' rose.

To go along with the June-blooming flowers of the 'Alchemist', I chose *Clematis* 'General Sikorski'. Its large, ocean-blue flowers will be breathtaking. Typical of most gardeners, I'm dreaming of the future, letting anticipation fuel my passion! Although I love the flowers and foliage of clematis, I've learned that many of them establish slowly, so patience is needed. I look forward to enjoying their rich colors and the many patterns they will make as their tentacles and flowers twist through the arbor and the rose.

For gardeners who have been hesitant to try climbers, I encourage experimentation. Do a small amount of research. Find out which roses you simply must have climbing in your garden. As years go by, when you are sipping tea on your patio, gazing at your rose, you will be happy that you took the plunge and bought a climbing rose.

CHAPTER FOUR

A Symphony of Blooms

THIS CHAPTER EXPLORES A POTPOURRI OF ROSES from various classes not yet discussed elsewhere. Some are old garden roses, which evolved prior to 1867, while the others are modern roses. We will tour through these roses as they are planted in my flower beds, visiting each gorgeous bloom in turn. Although many old garden roses only bloom once for a few weeks in early summer, others repeat-bloom. Some roses from Asia carry the trait to repeat-bloom, but in colder climates such as the Intermountain West, this capacity may be slightly diminished. However, many gardeners I know have had success growing these richly colored and perfumed repeat-bloom roses in the Rocky Mountain region.

Let's begin with 'Baronne Prévost'. I have only recently planted this rose, but it has been grown locally for decades and was introduced into commerce in 1842. If 'Baronne Prévost' is exceedingly happy—meaning it likes where it is planted—it can reach 8 feet in height with a spread of 4 feet. Generally, though, its growth will be more moderate, staying at about 5 feet. It produces gushes of scented rose-pink flowers that remind me of a ruffled taffeta dress a stylish lady might have worn to a ball in the nineteenth century. It blooms throughout the summer and sporadically in fall. Since it may get large, I have placed mine along a fence, where it will act as an excellent frame for many perennials and grasses.

A rose that I have grown for a number of years is 'Louise Odier'. Its luxurious, frilly full blooms, which repeat similarly to 'Baronne Prévost', but more abundantly in fall, are warm pink with a lavender tint toward the center. Thorns are not profuse, and once the flowers

'Baronne Prévost' rose, with pink to lilac-tinted flowers, produces large blossoms—sometimes almost 4 inches across—among stiff, vertical canes.

have faded, fall brings on shiny red hips that are teardrop-shaped like pendants on a crystal chandelier. These will hold fast onto the shrub well into March. Along with evergreens and dwarf bulbs, they decorate the often-dreary late winter/early spring landscape. I like 'Louise Odier's' vase-shaped open habit. Currently it is 5 feet tall with a spread of 4 feet. I suspect it may grow another foot or so, which is usually its maximum height. Winter damage on the canes is minimal. In early May, I snip off any dead or decaying branches, giving it a final once-over before it bursts into flower.

'Louise Odier' is situated close to the center of a large bed, not far from 'Therese Bugnet', a rose known for double reddish-pink flowers, which contribute to this vivid rosy scene. The ornamental grass *Miscanthus sinensis* 'Gracillimus' adds majestic flare at 5 feet high and wide. Another perennial massed nearby is the 15-inch *Stachys spicata purpurea*. Its wandlike purple flowers make it an excellent companion plant against the round rose blooms. Below these perennials is a

cushiony dianthus with a delightful name, 'Sops-In-Wine'. Its evergreen foliage is blue-gray, and the quarter-sized, mostly flat flowers are speckled crimson and white. They bear a nice spicy fragrance for those who can bend far enough to take a sniff.

A rose with intoxicating perfume is 'Rose de Rescht'. This rose was introduced to England, prior to World War II, but expert rosarian Brent C. Dickerson suggests it may date back to 1680. I've recently planted it in a newly made flower bed. I received it by mail as a small bundle, delicately wrapped in damp newspaper. Even though it had a long and rough journey and was laid over at a post office, it arrived safely with glossy green leaves and a few healthy stems. It had plenty of time to get established through the fall before winter winds and a carpet of snow blanketed the landscape.

'Rose de Rescht' has sensual, fuchsia-red pompon flowers with hints of purple, which grow in fist-tight bunches tucked close to its green foliage. It blooms somewhat consistently summer into fall.

The deep-pink blossoms of 'Louise Odier' rose harmonize well with the single, peachy blooms of Armenian poppy (*Papaver triniifolium*).

The darkish-pink blossoms of 'Rose de Rescht' are softened by a white geranium companion.

Over time, this rose becomes dense and may reach 5 feet high and wide. After snow and cold subsides, there is some dieback of its canes, depending on the severity of winter. Although one has to look out for suckers in subsequent years, this rose is a favorite of many rose lovers and is easy to grow. Since I am a devoted fan of ornamental grasses, I planted *M. s.* 'Graziella' nearby. This 5-foot grass has long slender foliage, topped by fluffy, off-white plumes, which contrast with the rose's expanded blooms and woody mahogany canes.

One rose that has been a slow, but easy and steady grower for me is 'Alfred Colomb'. Some garden writers have judged its strawberry-red double blooms loud and vulgar. Since the loud color fits right in with my bubbly personality, I am delighted to welcome this rose into my garden. Blooms come in summertime with some repeat in fall, when 'Alfred Colomb' flowers in concert with other perennials such as the frothy, large, white daisy *Boltonia asteroides* 'Snowbank' and the

ornamental grass *Deschampsia flexuosa* (crinkled hair grass), known for its dense, bouffantlike inflorescences, colored bronze to pale greenish yellow. In keeping with the loud flowers of 'Alfred Colomb', nearby it I grow *Echinops ritro* 'Veitch's Blue' (globe thistle). The plum-sized round blooms on the 4-foot-tall plant display the darkest shade of blue I have ever seen in a flower. For a startling summer bouquet, combine the rose with the globe thistle. 'Alfred Colomb', at about 3 feet high and wide, nestles near a winding path, where another perennial grows at its feet—a purple aster ('Professor Anton Kippenburg') that needs to be divided fairly frequently to prevent it from overwhelming the rose.

Not far from 'Alfred Colomb' is a rose I planted just a year ago, 'Sparrieshoop'. I hadn't remembered I planted it, so the following spring I bought another one. How lucky can I get?! 'Sparrieshoop' has been grown in my region for more than a decade, so I'm con-

The dark red, globular blossoms of 'Alfred Colomb' rose create a pleasing picture against a backdrop of greenery. The garish bloom also complements the profuse display of pink flowers in my "rose kingdom."

'Sparrieshoop' rose, with its glossy green leaves, is pleasing to admire when surrounded by a mass of lavender. (Photo courtesy of Bill Campbell)

fident that, with adequate mulching while it is young, it will survive our winters. This winning rose has been around for fifty years and is named for a village in Kordes, Germany, where the Kordes family has a famous nursery. Buds are plump and colored deep rose; the five-petaled flesh-pink flowers bloom in panicles and open so wide they seem to gobble up the sunshine. When rained on, the flowers will look spotty with red blotches, so, if possible, avoid overhead watering. Some books speak of this rose's sweet scent, yet I have not detected any fragrance. New leaf growth and stems on this repeat-blooming shrub rose are a glossy maroon, changing to dark green, which contrasts well when paired with the blossoms. Although draped with abundant prickles, they, too, have a reddish cast and are visually appealing. At the edge of this flower bed, in the shape of a half-moon, I have planted the low-growing *Geranium pratense* 'Plenum Violaceum'. This geranium's double mauve-violet flowers look like crumpled colored tissue paper.

Staying festive, I adore the brassy personality of 'Reine des Violettes' rose, whose French name reminds me of a striptease joint where sleazy characters might hang around. Instead of being with questionable characters, this fragrant rose with rich purple, blousy flowers is in the company of *Panicum virgatum* 'Dallas Blues' (switch grass). The ornamental grass, a fairly recent introduction, grows to 5 feet tall and wide, about the same height as 'Reine des Violettes'. Its eleborate plumes, which look like delicate cotton candy, are a foot high, 3 inches thick, and are lightly tinted purple. They sit upon 2-inch-wide, wavy blue-green foliage. This grass flutters in the summer breezes as it leans into the sturdy and erect canes of 'Reine des Violettes'. Come spring, I experience very little cane dieback on this rose and only need to randomly clip off an inch or two of brown cane.

I rarely water 'Reine des Violettes'—or, for that matter, anything in this back area of my garden. Basically, I'm lazy. It's too far to drag the hose and I want to keep the water use low here since I have a few silver foliage plants, such as *Atriplex canescens*, which might rot if overwatered.

Not far from this dry area is the first rose I purchased for my garden. A novice gardener, I first planted 'Variegata di Bologna' next to my neighbor's swath of grass. At that time, he proved his love of his green carpet by drowning it frequently with his sprinkler system. The globular, golf-ball–sized blooms of this rose never opened after the first year and then rotted, so I rarely enjoyed its crimson stripes on a creamy-white background. Eventually, I moved this 7-foot rose to a spot where it didn't receive any moisture other than what Mother Nature delivered. This rose's flowers are sparse, there is not much repeat-bloom, and it is prone to powdery mildew. Pruning it is no picnic either: it is very thorny and produces canes quicker than a jackrabbit. I'm waiting for a rose person who will take on the challenge of putting it in a "perfect spot," where it may thrive.

If I get a striped rose again, 'Camaieux' will be my choice. Although only a once-bloomer, it is a Gallica, which guarantees its fragrance and reliability in my region. When I see it in catalogs, I'm attracted to the purplish-pink and white very double flowers,

Right: With minimal water and attention, the tough, yet beautiful rose, 'Reine des Violettes' blooms on and off from summer into fall in a windswept section of my garden.

Below: 'Reine des Violettes' rose mingles with the yellow stems of four-wing saltbush (*Atriplex canescens*) and the greenery of various shrubs.

whose colors resemble a can of paint not completely stirred. Sweetly scented and compact at 3 feet, it would be perfect for a small sunshiny garden. Nearby, I would plant a perennial sage, such as the foot-high *Artemisia absinthium* 'Silver Frost' (wormwood), whose soft and spiky silver foliage would complement the cushiony flowers of the rose.

A rose that gives a stellar performance is 'New Face'. Its perky name piqued my curiosity. Planted adjacent to my patio, this rose has numerous delightful qualities. The creamy-yellow single blooms, edged in pink, are magnetic. Throughout its long blooming season—almost nonstop for more than three months—it sometimes has a few flowers that are either all white or all pink. All five petals are somewhat squared at the outside edge and each is spread a slight bit apart from one another—a distinctive characteristic not seen on many roses. The flowers come in voluptuous

Although a stunning striped rose, 'Variegata di Bologna' has been troublesome in my garden. Near the rose, I let the prolific annual mallow, *Malva sylvestris* 'Zebrina', emerge.

Left: The petals on 'New Face' rose are distinctively palm-shaped. Single blooms are a mixture of pink, creamy yellow, and white.

Right: 'New Face' rose, the flower in the center, mingles well with red-cupped Shirley poppies (*Papaver rhoeas*) and yellow meadow rue (*Thalictrum flavum* subsp. *glaucum*) in the background.

trusses and are wonderful when cut for an outdoor garden party in high summer. My plant reaches more than 6 feet and has a sturdy vase shape—quite narrow at the base, which makes it easy to prune or to cut out old canes. 'New Face' has sharp, but attractive deep-red prickles scattered along its smooth medium-green stems. I get a substantial amount of winterkill on the canes—more than 2 feet—yet this reduction never interferes with its superb performance once the heat of summer arrives.

When 'New Face' reveals its sprays of blossoms, a sea of flowers consort with it, elevating the overall beauty of my patio area. One of my favorite flowers to combine with it is *Papaver rhoeas* (Shirley poppy). I let this reseeding annual emerge wherever it chooses. The papery-thin red, pink, and white petals of this poppy soften the scene next to the stiff canes of the rose. To emphasize the many shades of red in this picture, I have added *Phlomis russeliana* (hardy Jerusalem sage). This statuesque perennial, tiered like a wedding cake, has dense whorls of buttery-yellow flowers spaced a few inches apart along its erect stems. At the base, large, floppy dark green leaves add to its appeal.

Closer to my patio is 'Nearly Wild' rose, an excellent choice for a smaller garden as it maxes out at 4 feet high and wide. Although not

'Nearly Wild' rose, a staple in my garden for more than a decade, produces vibrant, pinwheel-like pink and white flowers.

multicolored, the bunches of light pink single flowers with touches of white bear a close resemblance to 'New Face'. 'Nearly Wild' blooms throughout the summer into fall and has a light, pleasant fragrance. I hardly give this rose any attention since there is not much winterkill on the stems. After five or six years of almost no pruning, I noticed that it looked a bit scraggly. So come April, I'll cut out wispy stems, which won't produce any flowers, and remove some old canes that are past their prime. For a showy display, I've combined it with *Ratibida columnifera* ('Mexican hat'), with its protruding yellow or mahogany red-brown flowers and *Veronica incana* (silver speedwell), popular for its silvery-gray matted foliage, as well as its spiky violet-blue flowers. Once established, these three flowers will do well in a somewhat dry area; too much moisture will rot out the two perennials.

Another appealing rose for a small garden is 'The Fairy'. Popular since the 1930s when it was introduced, this rose can be outstanding used in the front of many perennials, such as delphiniums and *Achillea* 'Moonshine' ('Moonshine' yarrow). Alternatively, a massing

The popular 'Fairy' rose produces scores of rosette-shaped blossoms that are enhanced by bright green leaves. (Photo courtesy of Al Ford)

Left: The pale yellow flowers of Rose 'Golden Wings' is enhanced next to the orange long-headed poppy *(Papaver dubium)*.

Below: The bold reddish flowers of 'Alika' rose combine beautifully next to big betony (*Stachys grandiflora* 'Superba').

Blooming in big clusters, 'Marjorie Fair' rose is enhanced when the ornamental greenery of hardy pampas grass (*Saccharum ravennae*) winds among its stems and blossoms.

of these creates an easy-care ground cover. Each bush usually remains at 2 feet high and spreads 3 feet or more. Either way, 'The Fairy' has a prolific display of double blooms, which come in light rose-pink bunches on fairly long arching canes. It flowers quite steadily from late June into October.

'Nymphenburg' is a rose that has definitely reached its maximum height in my garden. This rose is another one of my star attractions, situated along a well-traveled path. Blossoms are almost double, loose, peachy salmon, and highly perfumed. 'Nymphenburg' blooms for a few weeks in June, with a smattering of repeat-bloom in summer. After eight years, the canes have thickened quite a bit and the thorns definitely say, "Keep back or face the consequences!" Aside from needing a few damaged or dead canes cut out here and there, this rose doesn't require much attention.

I like the growth habit of 'Nymphenburg'. Height-wise it is 5 feet, but its width is close to 6 feet, giving it an odd, but attractive structural appearance, as canes jut out in an unusual manner. Most are vertical, but a few almost-horizontal canes appear here and there. Beneath it, acting as a contrasting ground cover, is an ornamental grass—a Bromus (brome). *Bromus benekenii*, from Eastern Europe, is airy and low, with narrow, sand-colored panicles that curve gently down and wave about when winds blow. This wonderful grass's minor drawback is its aggressive nature. I always have a weeding tool handy to hack out the grass when it wanders where it is not welcome. After ten years, in spite of the hassle of containing this grass, I let it remain because it looks so picturesque as it skirts below the rose. This grass may be hard to find in the nursery trade because of its aggressiveness. *Helictotrichon sempervirens* (blue avena or blue oat grass) is a less invasive alternative.

Growing a combination of many perennials and annuals below or near roses softens and balances the woody structure of the rose. I have created this effect often, but in one spot I tried something slightly different. I have a very large grass, *Saccharum ravennae* (hardy pampas grass). It reaches anywhere from 8 to 12 feet, depending on moisture and location. Beneath it, on a spoon-shaped flower bed, are two roses: both are 'Marjorie Fair'. 'Marjorie Fair' is a low-growing shrub rose with a light scent. This rose is related to 'Ballerina', a pinkish-white rose that is thought to be borderline hardy in my region and that did not survive for me. However, I wanted to take a chance with 'Marjorie Fair'. Hundreds of people can tell you that a plant will never survive in your climate, and that you are living in denial by trying it. Don't do it, try something else they frantically advise. Still, stubborn gardeners (of which I am sometimes one) will attempt it, cross their fingers, and hope for success. We gardeners are experimenters. We might feel smug, proclaiming to ourselves and maybe to others, "Look what I can grow!" I want reality to live up to my imagination. What a picture: a sea of red flowers with a cinnamon-colored Eiffel tower of ornamental grass blooming above it! Over time, we'll see how well this scenario plays out.

The single pink petals of 'Vanity' rose, framed by medium-green leaves, are picturesque with their brilliant yellow centers.

A good way to get design ideas for your own landscape is to study other people's gardens. In addition, you can check out their plants to see if any of them thrill you and send you dashing to the garden center. This is how I learned about a particular rose. Tucked in among greenery, showing a few deep-pink blossoms, this rose was quite narrow from top to bottom, but easily caught my attention. I asked my host the name of this rose. "Oh!" she said in a unimpassioned manner, "that's 'Vanity'." I took note and eventually bought the rose. Because I hadn't mulched 'Vanity' sufficiently over its first few winters, it threw in the towel and died. A number of years later, I tried again and now have a small specimen of 'Vanity'. I know eventually it will reach 4 feet tall. The blooms begin as piercing, dark red, pointed buds, which emerge from healthy matte-green foliage. The mostly single blossoms, which appear in clusters, are shaped like mini-craters, dotted in the center with yellow stamens. It is not a big, bushy shrub, and because of its trailing character and lankiness, I planted this rose between two shrubs so it can lean into and be supported by them.

For a breathtaking scene, I planted masses of a snapdragon variety named 'Ribbon Pink' in the vicinity of 'Vanity'. This annual reaches 16 inches tall, with overblown pink flowers, which are splashed yellow in the center.

Yellow entered the picture again when I encountered 'Golden Wings' rose. A colleague in the rock garden club I belonged to felt that this rose had grown too large for his garden. I jumped at the chance to acquire it, since I had definitely entered my rose phase and had heard that 'Golden Wings' produced beautiful blooms. All I needed to do was come by his garden and dig it up—a simple task. When the ground had softened up and defrosted from the ravages of winter, I went by his house to get my new rose. It had been planted for three or four years, so the roots had not spread too far. He watched as I carefully dug out about a foot from the edges of the bush. I made sure not to disturb the roots, but to get as much of the rootball as possible, thereby almost guaranteeing that it would arrive in my garden in one piece. With care, I placed 'Golden Wings' in a large bucket, gave it a little water for the journey, and cautiously lifted it into my truck. I thanked my colleague as I dashed off for home to replant 'Golden Wings'.

Within a few hours, 'Golden Wings' sat pretty, perched up a few feet on an exposed berm, where it would be the center of attention. For the last six years or so it has been a trustworthy bloomer. It is one of the few roses I have that blooms from June almost into November, depending on fall weather conditions. Even though it catches a lot of wind where it is planted, this rose's flowers hold on tight, oblivious to the windy conditions.

'Golden Wings' is symmetrical and nicely fan-shaped. Its height matches mine—about 5 feet. Width-wise we are very different, since it spreads close to 5 feet. 'Golden Wings' has thick, reddish-brown canes: the winterkill on the stems varies from year to year. Sometimes a big cane will die back; other times, I only need to give it a light pruning. The thorns are fierce and pointed. Overall, this rose is easy

Above: The dark-colored flowers of opium poppy (*Papaver somniferum* 'Lauren's Grape') echo the brownish center of the buttery, saucer-shaped blooms of 'Golden Wings' rose.

Right: The green foliage of *Iris spuria* bends among the frilled blossoms of 'Sydonie' rose.

to care for: thus far there has been no suckering and every few years I just cut out the old canes as well as any spindly growth.

My pride and joy with this rose is the panorama it creates in concert with the distinctive flowers that surround it, such as *Papaver somniferum* 'Lauren's Grape' (opium poppy). Design-wise, I don't pay much attention to color combination or color wheel ideas. But I do know harmony when I see it. 'Lauren's Grape', an annual poppy that reliably reseeds (some folks might call it weedy), has delicate single, silky-purple flowers with blue-green frilly foliage. After the flurry of blooming, these poppies leave behind grape-sized seed heads, also colored blue-green, with long, rail-thin stems. The seed heads resemble small balloons.

Since 'Golden Wings' has open, airy spaces between some of its canes, I chose *Clematis viticella* 'Purpurea Plena Elegans' to fill in the gaps. Over the years, it has produced dozens upon dozens of rosy-purple flowers that have four distinct petals, plus a protrud-

The plush, purple blooms of *Clematis* x *jackmanii* twist freely amid the full flowers of 'Dr. J. H. Nicholas' rose.

ing small round ball in the center. These thread their way through the carpet of green rose foliage, showcasing true elegance.

The soft pink blossoms of 'Sydonie' make it another attractive candidate for this clematis to wind through. Its copious, tightly twisted petals and sweet fragrance are satisfying features. Of equal importance is the demeanor of 'Sydonie'. This rose produces many flowers in June and then repeats sporadically into fall. I'm also pleased with its compact 4-foot form, healthy green leaves, and the small amount of care it needs once winter has passed. Its low water requirements are also a blessing. Without a sprinkler system in my garden, many of my roses toughen up and adapt to reduced water, especially with my less-than-perfect watering schedule.

A final rose for this section, 'Dr. J. H. Nicholas' could be classified as a large shrub or short climber. A colleague of mine has grown 'Dr. J. H. Nicholas' for more than a decade. Among more than sixty roses, this is one of her favorites. She finds it vigorous: flower production is good from early summer into fall. She's pleased with the light and deep pink fragrant blossoms that appear in bunches and singly. It has a faint resemblance to a hybrid tea rose, but without the fuss of that variety. Foliage is dark green and leathery. After such a long spell in her garden, it grows to 8 feet tall with a 6 foot spread.

I love all my roses, no matter what class. As I meander among my various flower beds, I see snapshots of beauty. Through a combination of random shopping, a small amount of research, and following hunches and desires, I have brought much diversity to my garden. Each distinctive flower, bud, or stem becomes a part of a larger picture when partnered with fellow roses and other plant material.

CHAPTER FIVE

Rose Breeders at Work

F OR CENTURIES, PASSIONATE ROSARIANS have been breeding roses, crossing them with one another, to achieve desired characteristics: a more beautiful or more fragrant rose, and/or a hardier plant. Long before humans began their botany experiments, Mother Nature was breeding. Sometimes we know the results, but not the story. For example, in ancient times some single flowers became double, but no rose expert knows when, where, or how. At other times, we know a bit of the history. For instance, in the 1830s, an attorney, George Harison, living on a farm in New York, was credited with noticing a chance seedling that appeared in his garden.

The gushing yellow blossoms of 'Harison's Yellow' bonds with 'Nevada' rose, while a blue geranium accents the scene.

'Harison's Yellow' creates a brilliant effect in late spring, when it acts as a backdrop to the stream of flowers in my rock garden.

The rose, whose exact parentage is unknown, became known as 'Harison's Yellow'. It was later carried across the plains by home-steaders: to this day, it is still seen growing untamed across many parts of the West. No soil amending or extra water are needed for this variety. Mother Nature rises to the challenge, providing what is necessary for this rose's beautiful blooms and longevity.

In the past fifty years, rose breeders have intensified their efforts to produce hardy roses for colder regions of the country, as well as to create roses that have repeat-bloom and fragrance. Most recently, they've introduced roses that are easy to care for, disease resistant, hardy, and long blooming. There is something for everyone: tall and short varieties, ground covers, roses for hedges, and more.

Austin Roses

By the 1960s, rose breeders were hard at work. David Austin, an Englishman known for his long fascination with roses, combined the fragrance, beauty, and character of the old garden roses with the long-blooming characteristics and colors of the modern hybrid teas and floribundas. From that union, the Austin roses, sometimes known as English roses, were born.

I do not have a lot of experience with the Austin roses. I did grow one Austin rose, 'Queen Nefertiti', and I loved the abundance of yellow flowers tinted apricot that the rose produced. However, one day when I looked out my window, I barely had a stick left! In truth, I probably forgot to mulch or water it! Overall, I prefer the old roses, with their fascinating stories, even though some bloom only once.

In their defense, many Austin roses grow well in the Intermountain West although, as with some shrub roses, a certain amount of winterkill on the canes should be expected. Mounding them up with soil or light wood mulch over winter, and of course watering them, helps ensure these roses make it through tough winters. Long-term testing for superior hardiness will give gardeners more insight into the Austin roses' strengths, weaknesses, and adaptability to colder regions, especially in more rural areas where they are not protected by buildings, trees, and shrubs.

Many people adore Austin roses for their rich fragrance, beauty, and very full petal count, as well as because many of them repeat-bloom. The following have been successful in the Denver–Boulder area for five to ten years or more: 'Constance Spry', a lovely once-bloomer, which has a double soft-pink flower and a strong fragrance, and 'Abraham Darby', with repeating double apricot-blend flowers. In addition, the repeat-blooming 'Evelyn', colored apricot, yellow, and touched with a hint of pink, has lovely slightly ruffled petals. 'Mary Rose', with rose-pink blooms, only has a slight fragrance, yet is special because it starts to bloom early in the season and finishes late.

Beautiful Bucks

Buck roses were bred by Dr. Griffith Buck during his tenure at Iowa State University in Ames, Iowa, from the 1950s into the 1980s. From a friendly chat with Dr. Buck's widow, Ruby, I learned that Dr. Buck worked closely with rose breeders in Canada and researchers at the University of Minnesota. When he retired in 1985, his research material was turned over to the staff at the University of Minnesota. In fact, one of his roses, 'Applejack', is on the cover of the book *Roses for the North*, produced by the Minnesota Agricultural Experiment Station, affiliated with the University of Minnesota. Mrs. Buck also shared an interesting tidbit with me: her husband was allergic to the pollen the roses produced and for thirty years needed to take medication so he could continue to surround himself with the plants he loved!

The hardiness of the Buck roses is variable in the Rocky Mountain region—some perform better than others. Like the Austin roses, they need more testing over a five- to ten-year period. How do they withstand long, dry winters with little snow cover? Iowa and sections of the Midwest, where these varieties were bred, do not have these conditions. Regarding these roses, I can only speak

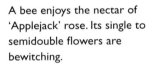

A bee enjoys the nectar of 'Applejack' rose. Its single to semidouble flowers are bewitching.

about the ones I've grown or the varieties that have been grown in my region for a few years.

Eight years ago, I snatched up 'Applejack' and have been very pleased with its performance. Although it doesn't exactly dazzle the onlooker, it blooms reliably and adds substance and structure to the garden. The modestly loose, rosy-pink flowers of 'Applejack', dusted in the center with yellow stamens, have a light apple scent. I have two of these roses within 6 feet of each other: they are given plenty of room. Their 6-foot vertical and somewhat arching canes overlap each other, which creates a pleasing effect. 'Applejack' blooms summer into fall, blending with various perennials I have planted around the rose. *Euphorbia palustris* (spurge) is a robust plant, with chartreuse flowers in spring that form a symmetrical mound that stretches 2 feet high and wide; in fall, the perennial is dressed in reddish and orange tones. To add vertical accent, I favor *Veronica spicata* 'Blue Charm', which blooms in early summer. I like its thickish, lavender-blue flower stalks, which soar skyward around the rose. Every few years, I remove a few pockmarked old canes from 'Applejack' and do a little trimming of spindly canes. It's not a high-maintenance rose.

A Buck rose that I planted recently is 'Prairie Flower'. I bought it because I liked what the tag revealed: single, cardinal-red blooms with a white center. Although I adore double fragrant roses of any kind, I'm a sucker for singles, and this Buck rose sounded wonderful. At a potential height and width of 4 feet, this is placed in a spot where it is not hidden by any other plants, so I can enjoy its blooms and slight fragrance that will come from June until frost. An easygoing, evergreen perennial to surround the base of this rose is *Iberis sempervirens* (evergreen candytuft). Recently, I encountered a design idea of planting a few low-growing roses in a large space and letting the candytuft crowd around them, which creates a vision of roses that appear to "float" gently above the puffy sea of white flowers.

Two other Buck roses that have been grown in my region for about five years are 'Earth Song' and 'Wild Ginger'. The double flowers of 'Earth Song' are deep pink with deeper copper overtones and carry a sweet scent. The blooms come in groups of five and ten and it repeat-blooms well. It has nice, dark green foliage and will stay about 4 feet high and wide. The leathery foliage on 'Wild Ginger' is also dark green. In addition, the bushy shrub is known to have a good resistance to blackspot and powdery mildew. Its large blooms are borne singly and in clusters. The fruity, fragrant blossoms are cherry pink with lemon yellow at the base of the petals. A colleague who is quite the rose lover reports that, after five years in the ground, 'Wild Ginger' has been a bit stingy when it comes to repeat-blooms, although it makes a good show in June. There is some winterkill on the canes come spring.

'Carefree Beauty', a long-blooming Buck rose that is widely distributed at garden centers in my area, is a solid performer here and throughout many parts of the country. 'Carefree Beauty' was given high marks by *Better Homes and Gardens* in the March 2000 issue as one of the top-ten reblooming roses. The fragrant flowers of this rose, which have twenty to thirty petals, are produced on a plant that reaches 3 to 4 feet high and wide. This rose would be great for a massed display.

Local nursery staff give the Buck roses mixed reviews because some of them have not performed well in certain sections of Colorado, such as on the exposed, dry plains. Many gardeners in the city and suburbs of Denver have had success with Buck roses and plan on trying more. I suspect the protection of houses, buildings, fences, and other structures, plus a few inches of wood mulch and winter watering, help these roses survive tough winters.

The flowers of the Buck roses are pretty, and the names are delightful and a bit quirky, such as 'Freckles', 'Fuzzy Navel', and 'Countryman'. Many of Dr. Buck's rose names are connected to his personal life, such as 'Golden Unicorn', which was the name of his paratrooper division during World War II. This year, I have planted 'Distant Drums', which has double rose-purple flowers, as well as 'Hawkeye Belle', which produced a few ivory-white flowers with petals tinted pink toward the center. Come fall, it even showed off a couple of hips. I'll give these roses extra protection in the form of 6 to 8 inches of compost around the base of the plant in November, together with some good doses of water during dry spells.

In addition to reading, perhaps doing some research, and visiting a garden center, be sure to see firsthand how these roses perform in your region and what they look like. Find out about parks or zoos or special areas in your locale that have significant displays of roses. For instance, check out plant material that surrounds the offices of your state extension offices. In some cities, rose societies find public places, such as restaurants, or even malls, in which they volunteer to do attractive mass plantings of roses along with companion plants. Old garden roses in particular can be seen growing at old cemeteries. Sometimes cemeteries welcome the help of volunteer gardeners in caring for their roses. Volunteering is one avenue for the rose lover to become familiar with the growing habits of old-fashhioned roses and to learn which ones would be ideal for their backyard garden.

In June, when most roses are at their peak, browse neighborhoods, cities, rural towns, and even abandoned sites. Many people who lust for roses have been known to knock on the doors of private residences to inquire about old roses in people's gardens, in hopes of obtaining a wonderful cutting. One important caveat: people should never cut roses from landscapes not their own, public or private, unless they have permission of the home or landowner. Many gardeners, such as myself, are happy to be generous in supplying fellow gardeners with the cuttings they desire.

Hardy Canadians

A group of roses whose popularity has swelled in the past decade are the Canadians. Most of these roses are winter-hardy down to minus 35 degrees, depending on snow cover, winds, and various other weather disturbances. Although some may have substantial dieback of the canes through winter, root survival is excellent, and these Canadian roses come up smiling and bloom in the summer. In addition, they have other traits that the consumer craves, such as the capacity to rebloom and flowers that have various amounts of perfume—although overall, the Canadian roses are not particularly known for their strong scents.

'Henry Hudson' rose appears elegant next to deep-green leaves and the pinkish bud below. (Photo courtesy of Bill Campbell)

One of the wild roses that has been used by Canadian breeders is *Rosa arkansana,* native to the north-central United States as well as portions of Colorado. This rose is known for its adaptability to cold climates and tolerance to hot, dry summers—in the mountainous West we can relate to that climate! Canadian breeders also drew on *R. spinosissima,* the species rose I described earlier that grows from Iceland to Eastern Siberia and also south into the Caucasus and Armenia.

'Henry Hudson', a hybrid Rugosa, is extremely hardy and has been tested down to minus 46 degrees. Its petite size—under 2 feet—makes it ideal for the smaller garden. I liked my first purchase so much that I bought another one to place in a far corner of my garden, at the base of a tall grass and around an annual verbena. The buds of this rose are light pink, with a slight point at the tip. Upon opening, the big fluffy white blooms are tinged pink. 'Henry Hudson' produces another flush of flowers in fall and has an enchanting spicy clove fragrance. Autumn color is at its peak in October as the entire bush turns golden and shades of orange, punctuated by succulent, soft red hips. (I did not find the hips tasty: I'll admire them visually and leave cooks and tea fanciers to concoct their elegant rose hip dishes.)

Two more carpet type roses out of Canada are 'Morden Snowbeauty and 'Morden Sunrise'. Both roses will stay under 3 feet in height in cold climates. Although white like 'Henry Hudson', the blossoms and foliage of 'Snowbeauty' are different. The leaves are smooth and dark green, unlike 'Henry Hudson' whose foliage shows more rugosa characteristics and therefore feels and looks rougher. The petal count of 'Snowbeauty' is about twelve, which gives it a delicate appearance. The shrub produces flowers in clusters of three to five flowers.

Rose lovers will adore 'Morden Sunrise' because of the combination of colorful blossoms produced on each single bloom, which has about eight petals. Each flower is a mixture of yellow, orange, pink, and white. The foliage is a dark shiny green.

Carrying hips but much larger in stature is 'Adelaide Hoodless'. I don't grow this rose myself, but it grows on my neighbors' property near their driveway, adjacent to a small garden of mine. These

Left: Watch out for 'Adelaide Hoodless' rose, whose broad, arching form can quickly overwhelm an area if not cared for properly.

Right: Glossy, dark green leaves complement the bursting red blossoms of 'Adelaide Hoodless' rose.

neighbors had helped me out, so I thanked them with a rose. (They had recently moved in and wanted something to zip up the dull narrow strip of white cobblestone.) According to local nursery staff, 'Adelaide Hoodless' was only supposed to grow 4 feet high and wide. However, as the old joke goes, plants don't read books. This rose has taken off, reaching more than 6 feet high and wide, with long, arching maroon canes that have astonished both my new neighbors and me.

These neighbors never water or care for this rose in any manner, unless the canes poke them when they enter or leave their vehicles, at which time they simply hack them back. In spite of this treatment, 'Adelaide Hoodless' thrives, blooming in July and repeating again briefly in September, a testament to its rugged constitution. The rose's many-petaled flowers have a light fragrance and come in large groups of deep red: they are excellent cut flowers.

This same neighbor admires my garden. Every so often she and a friend wander through and, upon seeing them, I give them a tour. On one of these tours, she noticed and liked 'J. P. Connell', thus far the only yellow rose released from the Canadian breeding program. She was delighted when, the following spring, I bought one for her. It snuggles contentedly by her back patio.

I've been growing 'J. P. Connell' for a few years. I like its winter dress. The canes are wine-burgundy, like a red-twig dogwood and

almost as smooth. I'm a tactile person; I like running my fingers up and down the canes of this rose and not having my hands mauled! Fall leaf color is vivid orange and red, and the hips are an unusual oblong shape. After winter has taken its toll on my garden, I often worry I will lose this rose forever since there is so much dead wood to prune away. Each spring, I prune it down to about a foot, yet it grows quickly and blooms in June with scented lemon-yellow flowers and large petals that resemble the fluted edges of a fancy piecrust. It also has a good amount of repeat-bloom later in the summer and the fall, not being bothered by excessive heat. So far, this rose is 4 feet high and quite narrow at the base. In gardens twenty miles from my house, the same rose has reached 6 feet high. I think the variability is due to the fact that in my garden, 'J. P. Connell' is very exposed, receiving high winds that occasionally come through my backyard. In other sites, nearby structures give the rose some protection from winds and other harsh climatic conditions.

When the flowers first open, their shape resembles hybrid tea roses with the familiar high centers, which should please gardeners who favor this style of roses. However, 'J. P. Connell' is much hardier and easier to care for than the hybrid teas. Although I am fond of this rose, I find its growth habit, which is vertical but leaning outward, rather awkward. I'm hoping that as it matures it will grow out of this adolescent phase and become more regal.

Left: The pale yellow flowers of 'J. P. Connell' rose are especially good-looking as they frame a brownish center.

Right: Black-eyed Susan (*Rudbeckia fulgida* var. *Sullivantii* 'Goldsturm') takes center stage when engulfed by the fine golden tips of tufted hair grass *Deschampsia cespitosa*).

Above: Despite the fact that it is engulfed by three different ornamental grasses, 'Morden Ruby' rose takes center stage.

Right: 'Morden Ruby' is surrounded by various perennials: yarrow, salvia, blue avena grass, clematis 'Proteus', and Lady's Mantle.

In my view, 'Morden Ruby' is a very regal rose. The name itself conjures up images of precious jewels. Although only lightly fragrant, this rose has other virtues, such as tiny flecks of white on the edges of its medium-red petals, which shimmer in the sunlight, and reddish stems during the growing season and in winter. There is also hardly any winterkill on the canes. The flowers bloom in baseball-sized, globular clusters, and they repeat throughout the season. Upon maturity, the rose reaches 4 feet high and wide. 'Morden Ruby' is situated in a large flower bed among many perennials and ornamental grasses. One ornamental grass in particular, *Deschampsia cespitosa*, has thin green plumes, whose colored tassels of silvery white look light as a feather and quite spiffy as they chaperone the rose. In addition, the thick leaves of the herb borage contrast with the shape of the rose, as well as the foliage of the grass. I also like the star-shaped blue flowers that dangle from the tips of the herb. When all these colors and textures magically combine, they create a feast for the eyes.

The paper blossoms of Shirley poppies (*Papaver rhoeas*) are a flattering complement to the candy-pink flowers of 'Morden Blush' rose.

Above: Climbing rose 'John Cabot' displays vivid red flowers among the delicate blooms of snow daisy (*Tanacetum niveum*).

Right: At the Denver Zoo, 'John Cabot' rose twists and climbs a sturdy split-rail fence.

Even though 'Morden Blush' doesn't open up with the power of 'Morden Ruby', the cotton-white, blush-pink flowers would accent any flower bed. Growing nearby is *Stachys spicata purpurea*, a 2-foot-high perennial with a few inches of purple, spiky flowers. This little-known perennial has an uncommon and pungent aroma, a counterpoint to the sweet scent of the rose. To create a layered effect, I planted *Thalictrum flavum* subsp. *glaucum* (yellow meadow rue) behind the rose. This meadow rue is topped off by small, cotton-ball mounds of yellow flowers. It reaches 6 feet high and 3 feet wide, dominating the rose and the betony. The meadow rue is quite prolific for me and pops up all over my garden. In a large garden, it makes a great background and accent plant for any bright-colored rose. Another perennial that I use often with many of my roses is *Knautia macedonica*. I'm fond of its small, round, pincushionlike red flowers, which would look nice engulfing 'Morden Blush'. (Incidentally, I have not found Knautia to be terribly aggressive in my garden. Moderate or low water use with many perennials is an important key to control the spread of plants that people want to contain.)

A bone-hardy rose that can stand alone or blend easily with other plants is 'John Cabot'. 'John Cabot' is well endowed with fierce thorns, so I'm cautious when I prune and weed the area adjacent to my patio where this rose is planted. The canes are thick and strong. Early twining around a sturdy trellis, when canes are more pliable, is recommended. My plant is still young, so I have time to sculpt it around the pole it is planted by. Although *Tanacetum niveum* (snow daisy) likes a bit less water than it is receiving in this area, it still looks divine, as its small white daisies with yellow centers seem to float all around the rose. Eventually this rose will reach about 8 feet high and wide, which is how large it has gotten at the Denver Zoo as it meanders along a 4-foot-high wooden fence. 'John Cabot' often has some winterkill on the canes, but that doesn't interfere with its flowering. The mildly fragrant, blush-pink, cupped flowers practically smother the plant in June and July; then they take a rest and bloom again in the fall. As the flowers wither, the petals hang on, changing to a pleasant shade of violet-purple.

Since many shrub roses repeat-bloom in summer or fall, many of them stop blooming for a stretch of time after their initial June flush. This rest may last from two to six weeks, a period during

Above: The raspberry-red blooms of 'William Baffin' rose are attractive when woven around a brick and concrete pillar.

Right: Pruned judiciously, 'William Baffin' rose is ideally situated in front of a wooden fence.

which they gather energy, form new buds, and bloom again. It is helpful for gardeners to remember that even though the rose may be repeat-blooming, blooms are often not continuous from June until frost. They have periods of rest. Also, if the bush is young, it may take a few years for it to offer the repeat sequence it is known for. And some roses will go dormant in extreme summer heat, above 90 degrees.

'Darlow's Enigma', the white, repeat-blooming rose I write about in Chapter Three, is planted near 'John Cabot'. These roses will make an attractive screen by the edge of my patio, blocking out the hot, afternoon sun that beats down on me when I entertain in the summertime. 'John Cabot' will be especially helpful because of its dense foliage; the leaves are smooth and slightly thick. To give more support to all these climbing roses, I will wrap turkey wire around three different poles, which are spaced horizontally 6 feet apart. As both roses mature, I anticipate the uproarious summer scene when they collide. In addition to 'John Cabot's' lavish floral display, its fall color is brilliant. The leaves transform into shades of orange and yellow that blend nicely with the green canes, creating an attractive, mottled effect.

I also like the fiery red rose 'John Franklin'. It puts on a nice show from summer into fall, when it blooms in clusters. The blossoms have many petals and it "dies" similarly to 'John Cabot', with the blooms fading to shades of purple before they finally gather on the ground. I take much pleasure seeing the hundreds of petals strewn on the ground in shades of white, purple, red, and more. The finished petals add sparkle and new dimension to the overall garden picture, especially when they fall on red flagstone, or colorful ground covers such as creeping veronica. I recommended this rose to neighbors down the street; they wanted something low and easy for their front garden. 'John Franklin' fit the bill. After five years, it has grown to 3 feet high and wide. Unconcerned with design or "correct" flower combinations, they unabashedly mixed pinks, marigolds, yarrow, and petunias, giving ostentatious color to this corner by their driveway.

'William Baffin' rose definitely fits into the category of flashy color. Wherever it is planted, it practically gains cult status! Its raspberry-red flowers with a touch of white toward the center and yellow stamens look as smooth and luscious as rainbow sherbet. The canes are vigorous, and in a sunny location the rose will reach an impressive 10 to 15 feet high and about 6 feet wide, with hardly any winterkill. This rose can be trained to climb or will provide a great thicket for privacy. After it becomes well-established in five or six years, 'William Baffin' will need to have its canes thinned out occasionally to reinvigorate it, assuring its good performance for years to come. 'William Baffin' does repeat-bloom, but not as intensely as its first flush in summer. For a rich planting scene—a scene Pierre-Joseph Redouté, the world-famous French flower painter, would have been proud to paint—add the vertical accent of blue delphiniums. To make the picture jell even more, add the once-blooming rose 'Madame Hardy', with its distinguished white blossoms.

'William Booth' is a Canadian rose unfamiliar to many people. Available only since 1999, my specimen has been in for five years. Highly thorny, it has long canes that reach out far and wide, likely to 7 feet. The robust branches can be trained to meander on the ground among other plants or climb a short trellis. The plant's single, red nonfragrant flowers bloom in clusters and, unlike 'William Baffin', repeat well into late summer. However you grow this rose, make sure to give it sufficient space.

Another Canadian rose that has impressed me in recent years is 'Cuthbert Grant'. When temperatures in Denver soared to 100 degrees, this is the only rose that offered up some blooms. Even though it is not intensely prolific in its blooming, I'm pleased with its satiny crimson petals and sweet fragrance. Canes shoot straight up; a few lean off to the side. Several references state that 'Cuthbert Grant' will stay under 4 feet: mine must be happy because it is 5 feet tall.

The final three Canadian roses I will describe are mere infants in my garden, planted barely a year ago. They have not had much time to sink their roots down, clench the earth, and explode, like fireworks, into flower. Because of their brief growing period, I rely on the reports of colleagues in my region who have more extensive experience with them.

Since these roses are grown in the cold regions of Canada, I feel confident they will be wonderful, prolific bloomers once they snuggle in. 'Winnipeg Parks', one of the smaller Canadian roses, has

Left: The red-cupped bloom of 'Cuthbert Grant' rose is velvety and luminous.

Below: The symmetrical, bold blooms of 'Winnipeg Parks' rose are softened by the relaxed, gray foliage of lamb's ears (*Stachys byzantia*) that pokes through.

become a hit with a colleague of mine, Tom the nurseryman. His eyes brighten as he rambles on about the virtues of 'Winnipeg Parks', which has been growing happily in his home garden for a number of years. He raves about its large, cherry-red blossoms and the fact that it starts out with pointed, deep-pink buds, similar to those of hybrid teas. But the similarities end there. 'Winnipeg Parks' is reliably hardy to minus 20 degrees. The lightly fragrant, cupped flowers, with about twenty petals, grow in clusters on this dense, short bush, blooming almost continuously from spring to fall. Although my plant is young, I have been able to admire the few flowers in addition to the shiny foliage that is tinted burgundy along the edges of toothed leaves, as well as through its veins. When fall comes around, since I'm crazy about yellow daisies, I'll plant *Rudbeckia fulgida* var. *sullivantii* 'Goldsturm' and the fast-growing and very tall *Heliopsis helianthoides* (false sunflower). This sunflower has been long-lived in my garden, requiring division every two or three years.

A rose that is taller than 'Winnipeg Parks' and that blooms in clusters of up to eight per stem is 'Frontenac'. This fragrant rose is named after the seventeenth-century governor general of the French-Canadian colony that stretched from modern-day Ontario to the Louisiana Territory. 'Frontenac' is extremely floriferous: the shrub is smothered with deep-pink flowers in June and continues to bloom substantially until late in fall, when a heavy frost terminates its beauty. My specimen is planted a few feet away from a flagstone wall. As this rose matures, I hope some of the flowers will sprawl and bend onto the stone, thrusting a rosy scene into the spotlight.

One of the most popular colors in roses is red. Of the more than forty roses produced in this Canadian breeding program, almost half would be considered red or a red blend. 'Cuthbert Grant' is a pure, velvety, dark red rose with many petals. Like 'Winnipeg Parks', the flower is shaped somewhat like those of the hybrid teas, whose form attracts many gardeners. The fact that it repeat-blooms in September and is nicely scented is a major asset for buyers. I was drawn to buy it because of its hardiness factor. After planting this 3-foot-tall rose, I did some research and learned that it has won many awards since its introduction in 1967, including the Award of Merit in 1970 from the Western Canadian Society for Horticulture. This rose's foliage appeals to me: its glossy, green leaves complement its grandiose red flowers, and the young canes are a pleasant shade of lime green. If you are a lover of red roses, 'Cuthbert Grant' is one to purchase, an ideal choice for any size sunny garden.

There are many other Canadian roses that perform well in northern regions and beyond. Most have various degrees of winterkill on the canes, but they come back to bloom prolifically throughout the season, needing only a minimal amount of winter protection other than snow cover. Try them. I guarantee you'll be pleased!

Roses by Meilland

Years ago, before other breeders jumped on the bandwagon to churn out roses the gardening public clamored for, there were roses by Meilland. The Meilland family, based in the south of France, has been breeding roses since 1898. Their most famous rose is 'Peace', a hybrid tea. It existed as a test rose as early as 1939. For history buffs, when the Meillands knew that France was to be invaded by the Germans, they sent plant material to nurseries in Italy, Turkey, Germany, and the United States. Each of these countries gave the rose a different name. It received the Portland Gold Medal in 1944, but was officially introduced and named 'Peace' in the United States at the Pacific Rose Society's spring show on April 25, 1945, the day the Allied Forces captured Berlin.

In addition to breeding many hybrid teas, this family created other well-known modern roses such as 'Bonica', an excellent low-growing rose known for its continuous sprays of cottony, pink, fragrant flowers throughout the growing season.

I became familiar with the Meilland family of roses when I purchased 'Ferdy' from a local grower about ten years ago. Technically speaking, 'Ferdy' is not a Meilland rose. It was bred using a Meilland rose as one of its parents, which is why it is classed with the other Meilland roses, but it was raised by a Japanese gentleman named Suzuki. I have been so pleased with my purchase that a few years back, after 'Ferdy' had become established and mixed with other perennials, I took a photo of it, framed it simply, and hung it in my office. When I give slide presentations on shrub

Left: The narrow, green stems of *Miscanthus sinensis* 'Yaku Jima' wind through the peachy-pink blossoms of 'Ferdy' rose.

Right: 'Butterfly Blue' pincushion flower (*Scabiosa columbaria* 'Butterfly Blue') is a delightful counterpoint to the fine-textured leaves and dainty flowers of 'Ferdy' rose.

roses, I often take this picture with me to let gardeners know how much 'Ferdy' epitomizes the spirit of roses.

In my exposed backyard garden, this rose stays under 3 feet in height, but the canes stretch out to nearly 4 feet. The peachy-salmon blossoms have about twenty petals, and they are highlighted toward the center with touches of yellow and white. A powerful flush of flowers blooms along the cascading canes in spring, with a smattering of color appearing again in summer. The polished green leaves are small, but appear in such abundance that they create a dazzling sight. Foliage color in fall is shiny maroon and plum.

While 'Ferdy' blooms in June, poking through its stems is the wispy greenery of *Miscanthus sinensis* 'Yaku Jima', one of my most treasured ornamental grasses. These grasses encircle 'Ferdy' on three sides. As visitors linger in my garden in June, I am constantly barraged with compliments for this rose. Located at an edge of a curved gravel bed, it cannot be missed. Because 'Ferdy' butts up to a path, pruning is an easy task. Every two or three years, over the winter months, I thin out old and decrepit canes. In early May, I prune it again, finally cutting out all the dead growth at the tips or wherever else I see very thin stems that don't look like they will be productive.

A Meilland rose that doesn't require much pruning or attention is 'Pink Meidiland'. Produced seventeen years ago, this lightly scented rose is widely sold at wholesale and retail nurseries. Its shape is upright, yet it remains under 3 feet high and wide. Single blossoms always catch my attention, and this one is no exception. The slightly cup-shaped flower with wavy petals is deep pink, with a sudden bold demarcation line near the center where pink changes to white. The small stamens add a touch of dark yellow. The foliage is quite attractive, too: the leaves are medium green and leathery with a bit of shine, a trait not common in shrub roses. Autumn brings about the appearance of pearl-shaped, orange-red hips, which stay on the bush throughout most of the winter, adding variation to the sandy and evergreen colors of this chilly season.

I have a few medium-sized grasses and other perennials that mix well with the short stature of 'Pink Meidiland'. Drifting over and above the rose in light winds is the narrow, green foliage of *Pennisetum alopecuroides* (fountain grass), which reaches a height of

'Pink Meidiland' rose, with its simple flower, peeks out among the blue spires of English lavender (*Lavandula angustifolia*).

'Sea Foam' rose basks in the sun as blossoms and glossy leaves droop on white granite rock.

about 3 feet. This grass blooms in late summer and has 3-inch-long tan and slightly pink inflorescences that, on a smaller scale, resemble foxtails. In fall, I'll be browsing this area and pulling on some of the seed heads, dispersing the seed far and wide. Kids of all ages enjoy this fun activity.

From afar, *Carex muskingumensis* (palm sedge), located on a corner near the rose, always garners positive comments from garden visitors. This symmetrical, olive-green grass gets a bit larger than the fountain grass and has wider blades, looking somewhat tropical, as its common name implies. In addition, in midsummer, many golden-brown flower spikes seem to squirt out of the center, which increases the beauty of this ornamental grass.

A final plant in this area is *Eryngium yuccifolium* (rattlesnake master). This sea holly (a common name for all Eryngiums) is native from New Jersey to Minnesota and south to Texas and Florida. As you can see from the states it grows in, this perennial is tolerant of a wide range of soils and temperatures. I grow it for its stiff, upright habit and attractive creamy-white, buttonlike flowers. I like the foliage, which has widely shaped bristles along the margins, reminiscent of yuccas. When all the plants in this area show off their striking foliage and flowers, a scene with great contrast in texture and color comes to life.

For an outburst of roses that are easy to maintain, plant 'Bonica' and the low-growing, award-winning 'Sea Foam', which has been around since the mid-sixties and continues to be a big seller at garden centers. 'Sea Foam' has lustrous, dark green foliage and blossoms that are creamy white, blooms in clusters, and repeat-blooms throughout the season. If space allows, plant a few of each rose, thus creating a mass effect and a feast for the eyes. Such a feast was produced at a local public garden when these two roses were used as a hedge in a long winding border. Since there were forty or fifty roses to prune, the head gardener was too overwhelmed to prune them one by one. His solution: trim them easily with a hedge trimmer in late April, down to about 10 inches. After this treatment, all roses came back and bloomed successfully.

Two more shrub roses of recent origin that I am delighted to grow are 'Flower Girl' and 'Flutterbye'. I came across 'Flower Girl' when I was on a shopping spree, buying my usual stash of perennials and other shrubs at a local wholesale nursery. The man in charge of roses, knowing they were a passion of mine, approached me. He asked me to try 'Flower Girl' and let him know how it performed. "Of course," I blurted out, and he handed me a bare-root specimen. I had never heard of this rose before, but I'm always willing to experiment with something new, especially a rose.

I planted it in my usual casual manner and then ignored it for several years, tending my other plants. Suddenly, one scorching summer afternoon, I looked up and there it was, blooming its head off. Wow! It was covered with voluptuous trusses of pink and creamy white flowers, dotted in the center with yellow stamens. Each flower begins as a pearly white bud, which, as it unfurls, turns a luscious pale apricot-pink and finally opens flat with about ten to fifteen petals. The blossoms emit a mild apple fragrance and the shrub blooms continuously from summer into the chilly months of autumn, when the bush is peppered with orangey hips that add zip well into winter. This vase-shaped shrub, narrow at the base, reaches about 5 feet tall. The strongly vertical, emerald-green canes are sparsely covered with thorns. 'Flower Girl' is planted where it rarely receives additional moisture, beyond the natural amount the Denver area is blessed with—which in most years is

Right: Blooming in clusters, 'Flower Girl' rose is enlivened by its deep yellow centers.

Below: The multicolored blossoms of 'Flutterbye' rose interlace with the lime-yellow florets of spurge (*Euphorbia seguieriana*).

about 14 inches. In back of this splendid rose is *Panicum virgatum* 'Dallas Blues'. The purple tints and airy texture of switch grass blend casually with the pastel blooms of the rose.

I bought 'Flutterbye' because the flower and its quirky name both intrigued me. The single flowers come in a multitude of colors, including yellow, coral, pink, and white. Some petals have a mixture of colors. The huge spectrum of colors on one plant makes 'Flutterbye' very eye-catching. Some people compare 'Flutterbye' to 'Mutabilis', another multicolored rose grown in warmer regions of the country where temperatures will not dip down to 20 or 30 degrees below zero. At the nursery where I purchased 'Flutterbye', in a highly visible demonstration garden, a few of them were massed together, presenting an irresistible display. I decided it was a rose I had to have. Currently it is 3 feet high, but over the years, as it grows, I suspect it may reach another foot or two. After winter has passed, it has only a few inches of winterkill on the canes. I'm also attracted to the polished green leaves that nicely surround the brightly colored blooms. At the moment, where this rose is planted, the ground is sparsely covered with just one perennial: *Scabiosa ochroleuca* (pincushion flower), which reaches 2 feet tall and is topped off by pale yellow flowers. In the future, I relish the opportunity to plant more flowers around this rose.

An excellent summer-blooming ground cover to gather at the base of both 'Flower Girl' and 'Flutterbye' is *Saponaria* x *lempergii* 'Max Frei' (soapwort). The lilac-pink, starlike flowers of this plant emerge from long, thin, tubular buds. To add pizzazz and more height to the bright-hued picture, I plant *Echinacea purpurea*.

A rose that will add a major splash of color to any flower bed is 'Knock-Out'. An All-American Rose selection from the year 2000, it is almost gaining cult status from beginning gardeners to the more advanced. It appeals to the masses because it's maintenance free, disease resistant, and is constantly in bloom from June until zapped by a hard frost. Stunning pictures reveal single, cherry-red blossoms, on a dense rounded shrub with healthy blue-green foliage. No deadheading is necessary: petals fall off easily, while more keep on coming. Colleagues have described it as a workhorse rose. It can take the heat at 90 degrees as well as chilly fall temperatures. A mature shrub will reach 3 to 4 feet

The satiny petals of 'Knock-Out' rose look somewhat Christmassy next to pointy dark green leaves. (Photo courtesy of Al Ford).

high and wide. Although only slightly scented, its major claim to fame is that it is touted to perform well given only two to three hours of sun. Because of 'Knock-Out's' popularity and adaptability, breeders have produced other forms of 'Knock-Out' such as 'Knock-Out' double pink and 'Knock-Out' blushing. If you grow the red form, one appealing partner would be the annual light pink 'Ribbon' snapdragon, with a yellow throat, which also tolerates some shade. In addition, since this rose is so successful in partially shaded sites, there are many more perennials to combine with it. Try the more familiar *Campanula rotundifolia* 'Olympica' (bluebell), which likes drier soils, or experiment and plant the unusual *Tricyrtis hirta* (toad lily) with its star-shaped, speckled flowers, which prefers a moister spot and benefits from mulching in cold regions when sufficient snow cover is lacking.

Speaking of mulch, if you wish to grow smaller roses in pots that are left outside all winter, then you must mulch quite heavily (3 to 4 inches of wood mulch) and water in winter, maybe every week or two if there is not sufficient snow cover. 'Gourmet Popcorn' is a good rose to try in a pot. It sports masses of petite white flowers, contrasted with a light splash of yellow in the center. This highly floriferous rose that blooms summer into fall will grow to about 3 feet tall and wide, with a cascading habit. Since this rose blooms so profusely, plant it near a bold, contrasting dark color, or place it near

Blanketed with blooms, 'Gourmet Popcorn' rose sparkles near a black wrought-iron bench.

various hard metals. Organic and inorganic elements, plus dark and light features, create a potent visual scene.

A shrub rose that has been quite popular in recent years is 'Starry Night'. Available since 2002, its pure white blossoms, highlighted with golden stamens, reach about 4 feet high and wide. Although it is scentless, it is a continuous bloomer from summer into fall. In addition, because of its beauty, disease resistance, and tough constitution, it became a winner in 2002 as an All-American Rose Selection.

In my eyes, the rose 'Raubritter' is spectacular. Even in its first year in my garden, it had a few double flowers, about the size of ping-pong balls and almost as round. Its flower opens darkish pink, fading to lighter pink. 'Raubritter' has a light scent and blooms once in early summer. This shrub is mostly a ground cover type, which can be used in similar fashion to 'Bonica' and 'Sea Foam'. I suspect in my region it will not reach more than 3 feet—but that is mere speculation at this time. Books have shown delectable pictures of this rose, which is what enticed me to buy it. However, a colleague in California has personal experience with this rose and finds that it is highly susceptible to mildew. Books also caution rose fanciers about this problem. However, I am hopeful that in my dry mountain climate, the rose's prognosis is better.

'Starry Night' rose is showy amid colorful pansies, as light and dark colors intermix. (Photo courtesy of AARS, All-American Rose Selection)

For an unusual background plant with 'Raubritter', try *Heracleum mantegazzianum*. Even in cold regions, it can reach 8 feet. Giant hogweed has massive white or slightly pinkish umbels, almost one foot across. The stems (or trunks) of the plant are as thick as small trees, ready to overwhelm anything in their path, so place it carefully. This uncommon plant is considered by some experts to be a noxious weed since it spreads with abandon. As contact with the plant may cause irritation and reddening of the skin, keep it away from children and be sure not to handle it without gloves! In spite of these drawbacks, I appreciate its distinctive features, especially when combined with roses and other plant material.

For me, growing 'Raubritter' and all my other roses is like having a pot of gold right in my backyard. I take tremendous satisfaction in stirring my pot often—tending the roses, taking in their scent, enjoying their colorful blooms. These roses need minimal attention, and are quite appropriate for people with busy lifestyles—or for any gardeners for that matter. Planted with care, offered minimal attention, and given correct siting, they will last for decades, bringing beauty and happiness to the homeowner.

CHAPTER SIX

Elements of Rose Design: Hardscape and Roses

ROSES BRING ELEGANCE AND EXUBERANCE to any garden. Whether you plant one rose, several, or dozens, the blooms, with their fragrance, texture, and fall color, add magic to the landscape. To determine the best situation for your rose, remember that most roses are sun lovers and require good soil and adequate drainage in which to thrive.

"Hardscape" is a landscape design term for inorganic structures, including stones, wood or stone fences, decks, flagstone paths, and anything made of concrete. Hardscape provides skeletal structure, the so-called bones of a garden. It also heightens garden appeal

Good soil is one of the key ingredients to help your roses grow healthy and happy.

A pea gravel path separates a rock garden from a perennial border. On the right is 'Ferdy' rose; in the back is the white rose 'Sea Foam'; far in the back is 'Hiawatha Recurrent' rose. Coppery foliage on the left is New Zealand hair sedge (*Carex comans*), along with trailing blue spruce (*Picea pungens glauca procumbens*).

with texture and shape, creating a visual balance between the artistic compositions of plants and nonliving elements.

The interplay of plants and hardscape elements needs to be somewhat controlled to prevent visual chaos. Hardscape structures provide a backdrop for plants, so they can cascade over walls and spill onto paths to soften the square, hard lines of irregularly shaped rocks and flat stones. Similarly, most houses have stark, rectangular lines that can be softened with the airier shapes of plants. For example, about 3 feet from the foundation of your house, plant a large shrub rose such as *Rosa eglanteria* (pink) or 'Lawrence Johnston' (yellow). Place a large round stone in front of the shrub, then intermingle various low-growing perennials with foliage and flowers that harmonize with the circular rose bloom. Randomly plant groups of salvia, penstemon, and veronica for

The climbing rose 'America' looks distinguished with the help of black shutters and the white brick.

vertical effect, and place clumps of sedum on one side of the stone. Since the perennials and the rosebush will take time to fill in, mass some annuals for instant color the first few seasons.

Plant material can also add structure to the garden. Shrub roses, like deciduous trees and evergreens, provide bulk, grounding, and solidity in the landscape. Rose canes, which may be thick or thin, vertical or horizontal, are more robust than annuals. Plant shrub roses anywhere you want a vertical accent or horizontal spray. Once the roses are in the ground, focus on different plant shapes that will blend and contrast with the round form of the rose blossom. Other plants will add softness against the angular, thorny canes.

Elevation change is another forceful design element. Changes in elevation create contrast and echo the flow of naturally hilly

Various perennials such as blue delphiniums, dianthus, and clematis highlight unknown roses.

geography. Even if your landscape does not have mountainous features, slight changes in elevation catch the eye. One simple way to create elevation change is to place several large boulders about a foot apart. You can enhance the effect by raising the soil level a foot or two. If you add soil, bury the stones about 6 inches to heighten the natural appeal. For a wilder look, plant the 'Harison's Yellow' rose among the stones. Its fragrant yellow flowers bloom only once in June, but this 6-foot shrub rose forms a pleasing thicket over time. If you desire a smaller, tamer rose, consider white roses such as 'Henry Hudson' or 'Morden Snowbeauty'. Both have fluffy white flowers and create a pleasant contrast to the red and black marble-like color of granite stones. Ornamental grasses or any sedum will provide architectural foliage accent to such a grouping.

If your approach to design is more intuitive, you may prefer to plant a shrub rose and see how the design evolves organically. Whatever your approach to design, the following ideas will help you to maximize the use of roses in your garden.

Location

Before planting roses in an existing garden, assess your landscape. Take note of sun and shade patterns as well as paths, structures, and trees. How does your house fit into the design scheme? Scale is important. While a large house calls for larger plants, a small house with large plants and bushes will appear overgrown, look out of scale, and be an eyesore. Become familiar with the locations of dry and moist areas in your garden, as roses don't like extreme desert conditions or continually "wet feet."

As you begin to brainstorm, it is helpful to keep a list or small notebook with ideas. First, you'll want to decide if you will design the garden yourself or use a professional designer. Either way, the following are suggestions for gathering ideas:

- Read garden and rose books and keep a list of your favorites.

- Visit public gardens: see what design schemes attract you. Are all the roses grouped together, or are they intermixed with other plant materials?

- Take garden tours in your neighborhood. Do certain arrangements pique your interest? Remember these, or jot them down. If you are drawn to a particular rose in bloom, ask the homeowner if she knows the name of the rose. Gardeners are often thrilled to share experiences with fellow plant people.

- Study plants in nature and mimic arrangements that appeal to you.

- Decide if you want to plant in your front, back, or side yard, then think of roses that could add the look you crave.

With an existing garden, you may wish to rethink and adjust some of the plantings. Eliminate plants that are difficult to care for or are growing poorly. If your garden is mature, you may have plants that have seeded around extensively. If you have more of a plant than you desire, prune or dig out the excess. Remember that plants can be moved and placement is not set in stone.

One more critical factor when deciding where to plant a rose bush is the space it will need to grow to maturity. Roses want room to sprawl and stretch out their canes. They bloom optimally, require less attention, and get fewer diseases when they are not crowded and receive good air circulation. To make this happen, learn something about the size of the rose you purchased. Either research the rose through books, talk to people who have grown it or to a knowledgeable rosarian, or, the very least, read the nursery tag. Once you've read the tag, I would still recommend giving the rose some extra space. You can always fill in bare spots with annuals until the new rose gains some size.

Matching Roses to the Garden Setting

There is a rose and design style to fit any garden situation. Whether your garden is large or small, full sun or part shade, roses add an artistic dimension to your landscape. Perhaps you want a hedge to separate your property from that of your neighbor. You could use low-growing shrub roses, or, if the site calls for it and you want a more dramatic statement, plant larger shrubs between the two landscapes. Over time, several roses planted together will create a mass effect, adding the new dimensions of height and density. In addition, roses add to privacy and provide a comfortable rhythm for the eye to follow. Once you've planted the hedge, you may enjoy it so much you'll want to repeat the pattern somewhere else on your property. This basic design principal of repetition helps to knit the garden together so it appears intimate and more inviting.

If you want a low-growing rose hedge with plants under 4 feet high, options include 'Winnipeg Parks', 'Morden Snowbeauty', 'Bonica', and 'Sea Foam'. 'Winnipeg Parks' and 'Morden Snowbeauty' are Canadian roses, which will withstand temperatures down to minus 20 degrees. 'Winnipeg Parks' is a dense bush with bright red flowers and dark green leaves: when mature, it appears as a drift of plants. 'Morden Snowbeauty' creates a similar effect and has ivory flowers. 'Bonica' and 'Sea Foam' roses are both long-popular choices for American gardeners. Both roses repeat-bloom and are lightly scented. 'Bonica's' pale pink blooms have more than thirty petals, while 'Sea Foam' offers waves of full, puffy white flowers. When planting roses in a hedge, you may choose to plant all one color or mix colors. From a design standpoint, a single color makes a stronger visual impact.

For a bold statement and larger hedge use 'Adelaide Hoodless', 'Charles de Mills', or *Rosa eglanteria*. All three roses reach 6 feet or more and make a dense hedge. 'Adelaide Hoodless' is a Canadian repeat-bloomer with red flowers. 'Charles de Mills' and *R. eglanteria* are one-time, early-summer bloomers. 'Charles de Mills' has red flowers, while *R. Eglanteria* shows off a profusion of single pink blossoms. After the roses finish blooming, their green foliage and stiff bending canes add vertical interest and form to any garden setting.

Whether you favor large or small roses, all roses are enhanced when planted among other flowers or shrubs that lend textural variation and hide the bare bases of larger roses. The globular form of rose blossoms partners well with the straight lines and colorful flowers of veronica, salvia, and penstemon. Contrast your roses with any plants whose flower shape differs from the rose flower. One noteworthy group of plants to use with roses is ornamental grasses. Grasses come in a wide range of shapes and range in size from under a foot tall to 12 feet. Their repetitive lines, airiness, and unique floral plumes complement the round form of roses, while the soft delicate features of grasses play beautifully against the thick masses of rose canes.

Another significant group of plants that augment the beauty of roses are gray- or silver-leafed plants. Silver sage (*Artemisia cana*) is an excellent choice among larger roses. This low-growing shrub has a rugged and natural look. The small leaves are feltlike and, when rubbed between your fingers, are pungent. For a softer appearance, plant the 3-foot-tall sage 'Powis Castle' (*A.* 'Powis Castle'). The lacy foliage forms an eye-catching mound.

In late summer, my blue house and pea gravel path create a stage for the tall feather reed grass (*Calamagrostis* x *acutiflora* 'Karl Foerster'), the bending plumes of brome grass (*Bromus benekenii*), and an unknown red minirose.

Large shrub roses are perfect partners for sunny, blank walls, where many feet of wood or brick create an empty canvas. Bring the area alive with shrub roses! A drought-tolerant, easy-care rose adds flare, height, and artistic shapes to empty areas. Choose a rose that will not overwhelm your site in terms of height and width, but whose leaves, flowers, and stems bring liveliness to an otherwise drab location. One selection is 'Banshee'. The fragrant pink flowers and long reddish canes of this rose would tumble away from the wall and provide a welcoming floral bouquet. If the wall or brick is a dark color, try 'J. P. Connell'. The double flowers of this variety are pale yellow, practically a creamy white, and contrast nicely against a dark background. If your setting is spacious near an empty wall, consider 'Martin Frobisher'. This rose suckers considerably and, over several years, will form an attractive thicket.

Garden Rooms

Well-designed landscapes create a balance between shady hide-aways and open vistas. Garden rooms provide comfortable private areas. A garden room, like rooms in a house, has a floor, walls, and furnishings (the plants). The walls or framework of a garden room are an important design element. They may be "green walls" in which roses may actually form all or part of the wall and serve as a backdrop for other plants, sculpture, or furniture. Garden rooms can create mystery and surprise. Imagine how delightful it would be to come upon a round engraved stone or the scent of a rose as you turn a corner! Put a bench in a secluded area: grow a shrub behind it or plant a row of roses to block it off, and you have created a garden room that pleases the eye and extends indoor living space into nature.

While on a trip to England, a fellow traveler and I sit on a famous white bench with the pink Austin rose 'Constance Spry' billowing behind us.

A rose hedge is a great way to separate different areas in your garden. Hedges work between a vegetable garden and your perennial border, between a driveway and the neighbor's yard, and around patios or decks. As you begin to lay out your plans for different design features in your garden, one idea will unfold into another and another. Soon, each area will have its own designated role and character, just like the rooms inside the house.

Roses as Specimen Plants

In addition to working well as hedges or in groups, roses are fabulous specimen plants. A specimen plant is one that is showcased in the garden in a stand-alone way. Roses, with their beauty and strong structural nature, invite the gardener to use them as focal points.

Roses are excellent specimen plants for flat areas. Picture a flat area scattered with various ground covers. Woolly thyme (*Thymus pseudolanuginosus*) carpets the area with lavender flowers in June and adds a pleasant scent. Blue fescue (*Festuca glauca*) adds grassy accents with bunches of blue foliage. Soapwort (*Saponaria ocymoides*), with its bright pink flowers and semievergreen foliage, has a spreading habit. Several shrub roses, loosely planted toward the rear or planted artistically off-center among the low-growing plants, will anchor the setting and provide color contrast and upright interest.

When roses whose canes have a pleasant open and spreading habit are planted in small groups among ground covers, they simulate a spray, looking like a dry waterfall. 'Meidiland' roses are perfect for this use and are easy to find at garden centers. Originally bred in France, these roses come in various colors and heights and bloom continuously and grow on average from 3 to 4 feet high. I'm partial to 'Pink Meidiland', which boasts a blotch of white in the center of five pink petals. The stems are sparse, but this rose has red hips that stay on through early winter. Another low-grower is 'Red Meidiland', whose clusters of flowers pump out color all season. 'Red Meidiland's' canes extend 5 feet and remain low to the ground. An eye-catching scene emerges as the rose canes stretch onto the woolly thyme and through the foliage of

the blue fescue. In addition to the 'Meidiland' roses, the Pavement collection also works well among ground covers. Popular since the late 1990s, Pavement roses stay under 4 feet tall and come in shades of ivory, purple-magenta, and various hues of pink. Exceptionally tough roses, they add vertical interest and color as they pop up through ground cover.

Larger and more dramatic shrub roses also work well as specimen plants. I have a small, egg-shaped flower bed surrounded by grass on one side and pea gravel paths on the remaining three sides. This bed gently rises 2 feet in elevation then tapers down toward the paths. 'Golden Wings' rose perches in the middle of the

A split-rail fence and a house in the background assist in accenting the white Alba rose 'Semiplena', while on the far right, yellow meadow rue (*Thalictrum flavum* subsp. *glaucum*) blooms. Yellow foxtail lily (*Eremurus* sp.) is on the bottom left.

flower bed. Although other smaller plants also call this spot home, the rose's distinctive characteristics make it an admirable specimen. Its thick branches curve down slightly and the big, butter-yellow blooms dip down gracefully near flowers scattered beneath the rose.

Designing with Climbers

Climbing roses conjure up images of English castles, weddings, and paradise as they trail, climb, and spill over fences, walls, and trellises. Any shrub rose with lax canes can be trained to climb. Climbing roses are immensely versatile. These shrubs can add upright accents to the garden or can meander along the ground and over walls. They camouflage unsightly buildings, soften hard lines, and paint the sky and garden with scent and color.

Imagine the possibilities. Let the white 'Alba Maxima' rose climb up a stark metal arbor. In several years, its thick canes will hide much of the metal and visitors will see only a profusion of white blooms. Let a rose such as 'Hiawatha', with its red and white flowers, trail along an extended 2-foot-high rock wall. The long, pliable canes of 'Hiawatha' can wind onto a path in front of the wall, gather on the ground, or poke through natural openings in the wall. To make the scene even more dramatic, plant a few silvery plants among the stone, such as the small sage 'David's Choice' (*Artemisia pycnocephala* 'David's Choice'), or use the larger gray-leafed sage 'Powis Castle' (*A.* 'Powis Castle'), which will billow over the wall. To create a striking front entrance, consider the rose miniclimber 'Jeanne LaJoie', which may reach 8 feet. Although its pink flowers are small, they produce a huge display. Plant 'Jeanne La-Joie' 5 feet from the front door. As it matures, train it through any solid support, such as turkey wire. Plant mounds of white and pink petunias at the base of the rose, and your front entrance will display a profusion of color throughout the growing season.

Roses in Winter

Interest in the garden does not evaporate when a heavy frost nips the flower buds, turning bright colors brown and, if we're lucky, coating the landscape in white. In my mountainous region, there are many warm, sunny days to walk in the garden and enjoy the natural woody structure of shrub roses against the sky. Shrub roses, with their thick colored canes, thorns, hips, and sometimes tangled growth habit, add winter interest after the leaves fall.

Rose canes, whether green, red, or tan, create picturesque scenes as they interweave with ornamental grasses. In one of my flower beds, I grow the rose 'Morden Ruby'. In winter, its firm red canes glide through the often-evergreen grass blue oat grass (*Helictotrichon sempervirens*). Rose canes are especially attractive when large ornamental grasses in the background move in the winter winds. Sometimes the rose and the grasses come together to create an intriguing entanglement. To create this effect, plant three dwarf maiden grass (*Miscanthus sinensis* 'Yaku Jima') in a half-moon shape. In the center spot, several feet away from the grass, plant any large shrub rose, such as 'William Baffin', 'Adelaide Hoodless', or 'Applejack'. The tan, flowery plumes of the grass, with their fine-textured thin lines, juxtapose stunningly with the stout, colorful rose canes. As winter ebbs and flows, snow adds an attractive component as it settles on canes and foliage.

Many roses adorn the winter garden with rose hips. Round or oblong in shape, most rose hips are shades of red. Some roses, such as 'Dortmund', *Rosa eglanteria*, and 'Linda Campbell' bloom in clusters, and leave five, ten, or fifteen plump red hips dangling together, creating a visual magnet in the garden. When any sandy-colored grass rhythmically sways in the background, rose hip interest climbs dramatically.

Walking through my flower beds on a winter day, I can closely observe the hips, stems, and thorns of many varieties of roses. While winter in the garden may not shine as brightly as spring, summer, or fall, it still creates a pleasurable tingle.

CHAPTER SEVEN

Maintenance Matters: Planting, Pruning, and Pampering

Planting a Rose

When planting any rose, first choose a site with at least five to six hours of sun. There are roses, such as the once-blooming Albas, repeat-blooming Rugosas, various species roses, and some climbers, which do well in less sunlight—roughly three to four hours. Generally, most roses, if planted in too much shade, will produce sparse blooms and leggy canes as they reach for the sunshine. Also, they may be more susceptible to diseases.

Roses are grown in two ways: either in the ground or in containers. Suppliers who produce field-grown roses must dig them when dormant and ship them bare-root in late fall through early spring. Your local neighborhood garden stores usually buy from bare-root suppliers, then pot the roses on-site for sale. Suppliers who offer container-grown roses can ship them year round in the containers or offer them as bare-root plants in the dormant season. Container-grown roses tend to be smaller than those that are field-grown, and grafted roses tend to be larger than own-root roses. They will all reach the same size eventually. If you have ordered bare-root roses, check them immediately upon arrival for dehydration. If the "skin" on the canes looks shriveled, it is a good idea to submerge the rose in water for twenty-four hours.

Whether you plant a container rose or one that was mail-ordered and that arrives flat, flimsy, and small, the planting process is essentially the same. For roses purchased in containers, dig out a hole about 2 feet deep and wide (larger if your rose comes in a five-gallon container). Mound the removed soil near the hole.

Have ready a mixture of soil amendment, such as cow manure and compost, EKO Compost (a brand of compost made of brown and green wood products and biosolids), topsoil, etc. If you are new to rose gardening, check with a knowledgeable nursery person regarding a good soil mixture for your region. The soil mix should be two-thirds original soil from your site and one-third soil amendment. The amounts do not have to be exact—this general balance will work for most roses.

If you are planting a container-grown rose, remove the rose from its container, even if it is one of those supposedly biodegradable containers. (Some gardeners have been disappointed that these containers can take years to decompose. In the meantime, the roots on your rose are cramped and confined). Some roses slip right out of the container. If recently potted up, the soil will fall away from the roots. Don't be alarmed by this. If roots are tight or the rose has been in the pot for some time, removing the rose can be more challenging. If I can't easily budge the rose out of the pot, I have often forcefully pushed on the pot with my hands and have even stepped on the pot to free a delectable rose! You might even have to resort to cutting the pot down two sides. Do whatever it takes. After prying roses out of their containers in whatever manner is required, I have never lost one—and I have planted hundreds of them. Most plants are tough and resilient. If I see that the roots are very knotted and tight (not a common occurrence with roses), I may take a sharp tool and slice into the bottom and side roots a few inches to loosen the root-ball, thereby encouraging the roots to spread out and become easily established in the ground. My next step is to throw a few shovelfuls of soil into the bottom of the hole, then smooth it over lightly with my shovel or hand. Next I place the rose in the hole, 3 to 4 inches lower than ground-level. For all my roses, I keep it simple and plant a bit deeper than usually recommended, which may add protection in areas of the country with harsh winters. No damage is done, and I give the roses an extra boost for success (imagined or real) in their early phases of development. If your rose is a bare-root one, shape the soil into a little mound, set the rose on top of it with the roots draped down the sides of the mound. Now shovel soil back into the hole, alternating back and forth between the original

soil and the new soil amendment (unless you have premixed your soil and the amendments). Press down gently around the rose to eliminate air pockets, and add more soil if need be to fill in any gaps. At this stage, water the rose well. Once the water is added, the plant and soil will sink somewhat, and you may need to add a few more shovelfuls of soil and then water again. Early care of the rose—meaning sufficient water—is critical to its development. However, do not overwater at this time, as roses do not like "wet feet."

From my experience, the main difference in treatment between smaller mail-order roses and container ones, at least in the early years, is winter protection and sufficient water. Most 10 or 12-inch mail-order specimens definitely require winter protection, especially in cold regions of the country: otherwise the rose will likely die and you will be left with a brown stick. Around Thanksgiving, I shovel some soil amendment on top of the rose, going up 8 to 10 inches, and let the soil easily fall around all sides, making a little cone-shaped heap. Regardless of what type of rose or where it was purchased, keep an eye on your rose, especially in the early years of its development. The time when the rose is anchoring to the ground is most critical for its healthy development. Top growth may develop slowly, but if all goes well, a lot of growth activity is happening underground. In roughly three to six years, your rose will take off and become the natural beauty you want it to be. Make sure it receives sufficient moisture during this period, but avoid getting overly generous with the hose. How much is enough? This will vary, depending on your soil, weather conditions, and region. I never measure the water consumption of my roses. I try to get a feel for the plant. I pay attention to the appearance of leaves, stems, and flowers. Sometimes I'll poke my finger down a few inches to judge how dry or moist the soil is. Drooping foliage or dusty dry soil tells me the plant needs a generous drink. If the soil consistency is muddy and wet, that indicates backing off on watering for a while is a good idea. Many roses, once they are established, are tolerant of some degree of drought.

When you move an existing rose bush, dig up as much of the soil and root-ball as possible. Transplant in late February or March, as soon as the ground thaws somewhat, yet while the plant is still dormant. Prepare the new site, amend the soil properly, and plant the rose. The roots will easily become established in the plant's new home. Whenever you move a rose, water it in thoroughly in its new site and remember to give it moisture on a regular basis as it acclimates. The important thing with roses, as with any part of the landscape, is to give consistent and continued attention to what you are growing and not just to plant and ignore.

To Prune or Not to Prune

Pruning roses is a much-debated topic. Each book or rose expert will recommend techniques and approaches that need to be followed to a T: cut the cane at this angle, but not straight across, which may damage the bush and contribute to disease. Cut exactly here, but not there. Use only *this* tool. Disinfect the tools and keep them clean and sharp. Prune precisely at this time of year, no later or earlier. Thanks to more and more rules from more and more experts, pruning roses begins to seem too complex and intricate. Perhaps the bush will say "Ouch!" or yell back that you messed up and that it's going to throw in the towel and die!

All this fuss is antithetical to my easygoing style of gardening. What is sorely forgotten in all these rules is why most people garden in the first place. From my point of view, we do it for beauty, fun, and fragrance. Perfectionism doesn't fit the gardener or the garden. We need to achieve a balance between pruning knowledge, common sense, and keeping to the general growth habit of the bush.

Patience and experience are most important tools for the rose gardener. Little by little, as with any endeavor or newly tackled job, the gardener becomes more skilled and trusting as she gains experience with roses, which increases her confidence. It helps to have a few guidelines from experts to achieve the vigor and flowering performance of roses, but let's stop there. Many people just like to putter, connect with nature, take pleasure in a few colorful, fragrant roses, and relax in the garden. The world has its share of stresses: pruning roses need not be one of them.

Unless you're tending very wild gardens, most roses need care and pruning. If they do not get some care, they become a tangled

mass of canes or tall poles, which in most cases, gradually only produce a smattering of flowers. Pruning encourages continued production of flowers, contributes to the overall health of the rose bush, and keeps pests and diseases at bay. Unsightly dead canes are cut out, which lets more sunlight into the center and contributes to better air circulation. Pruning stimulates new growth to emerge once old canes are removed or dead wood is cut out. Pruning also keeps a rose from exceeding the boundaries of its allotted garden space, so that one can walk past a rose bush along a path, enjoy its fragrance and beauty, and not be jabbed or bloodied by annoying canes and prickles.

Roses are very forgiving. They will survive poor cuts, some diseases, harsh weather conditions both in summer and winter, bouncing back to put forth healthy, beautiful blooms. As your rose develops and calls out for some attention, be ready to take on the task of pruning without too much trepidation.

Early Stages of Pruning

On average, newly planted roses will not need much pruning in their formative years, roughly the first three to five years. Spindly or broken canes and dead tips need to be cut out. If I feel it is needed, I'll also trim the rose back slightly to give it a somewhat tidier appearance. Then I will sit back and wait as the shrub anchors itself to the ground and watch while the canes develop above ground. Most gardeners want instant results. In a year or two at most, we wish for fountains of beautiful, fragrant flowers. Plants take time to mature. In practically every class I teach, people tell me about roses that have not grown much. They want to know what the problem is. I make inquiries as to location, sun, soil, and watering practices. Everything sounds fine. Many times, the reason for a rose's lack of growth is it simply has not been in the ground long enough! A familiar saying among gardeners is: "The first year it sleeps, the second year it creeps, and the third year it leaps." With roses, we need to remember that the rose may not leap at three years. Some roses are slow initially, but their growth spurts arrive later.

Pruning Once-Bloomers

Overall there are two approaches when pruning once-bloomers, which bloom for a few weeks in early summer and then provide a backdrop of foliage to any flower border.

Most often, the best time to prune is immediately after the single flush of summer flowering is over. In the Intermountain West, this means late July and August. If you prune in this fashion, new growth has enough time to ripen to the point where it will produce flowers the following year. How much to prune varies depending on the rose's location, how mature it is, the look you want, and how much it has grown this particular season. This is a subjective and aesthetic call on your part. Trim off the old flowers down to five leaflets. Go down the stem until you find the first leaf that has five leaflets and make your cut just above the leaf. If you want to reduce the overall size of the bush some or make it more compact, then go down a few inches to the lower leaves and make your cut there. However, if the plant is many years old or has not been given adequate attention, you may want to reduce its height more severely by cutting off 6 inches of growth on top or maybe even a foot or two. For an attractive specimen, I think it is a good idea to follow the general shape and character of the rose. There are no hard and fast rules to this. Don't worry too much and trust yourself: like your roses, you will get better over time.

If the rose produces pretty hips, you may want to enjoy these into winter: hence, you don't prune then. Also, in summer it is much harder to see what you're doing because all the leaves are still on the bush. Or this early pruning method does not fit into your gardening schedule. For instance, you're busy in summer with planting, weeding, and building flower beds. The heat takes it toll on me in summer. Therefore, I curtail pruning until a warm winter day, when I'm tired of the lacquered-looking red fruits. *At that time, with all once-bloomers, you'll not want to cut off too much of the top growth because then you will be eliminating the flowers for the coming season.* You can thin out a few old or thick canes, weighing the situation as you go along, deciding how much bloom you want to sacrifice. Whether or not to leave an old cane for this year if it is still producing flowers is a gardener's subjective decision.

Look out for canes that are too close to or rubbing one another, which will cause damage. When I do any kind of pruning, I do it gradually and slowly, inspecting the plant at different stages and from different angles and evaluating whether I want to make more cuts or perhaps wait until next year. Some years, you may prune the shrub severely: at other times, just the tips will do. If you're in a time crunch or get busy with other activities, you may skip a year all together! Most likely, the rose will survive and bloom just fine in summer.

From November onward into the following year is when I perform most of my major pruning tasks. With both once-bloomers and repeat-blooming roses, I browse my garden, checking for roses that need to be thinned or shaped. Are they too crowded? Is enough air and sunlight getting into the center? I look for the basic three Ds—the Dead, Diseased, and Damaged. I eliminate the entire cane or parts of the cane on afflicted roses. I also check for crossing canes, twiggy growth, or canes that are very old, pockmarked, and strongly discolored, a usual indication that the pith, the center of the cane, is injured. Healthy pith is a uniform greenish white. If the center of the cane shows yellowing or browning, it is damaged and should be cut back further. When I prune canes down, I try to be careful and not injure the adjacent newer growth. Sometimes this is difficult because rose canes grow close to each other. If a new cane is injured, I don't fuss too much because I know there will always be more canes coming.

I prune in this fashion through most of March. In April, as new growth begins to emerge and canes green up, I am overjoyed. I feel like I'm watching a football game and the quarterback has just made a touchdown. At that moment, the cheerleaders are going to start jumping gleefully, which is how I feel when I see the few inches of bright green foliage. In late April or early May, depending on weather and frost predictions, I'll begin to get more vigorous with my pruning techniques. I do not do heavy pruning before these times, because cold temperatures may still arrive. If I start too early and we then get a heavy frost, new growth gets zapped. By early May, I can easily see the strong demarcation between the new growth, which is green or burgundy and coming along strongly, and dead growth. I'll begin to pull back any compost or mulch that I have mounded up around the rose. Then I prune off all dead growth, cutting an inch or two into the new canes. I'll remove any damaged or diseased canes, then give the roses a final check. Each rose will be different. Some have extensive dieback, often a few feet. Others lose just a few inches on the tips of their canes. And some experience no winterkill at all. Throughout the spring and summer, I inspect my roses, seeing if I missed any old canes or if a rose has gotten too big for its spot. Even at a so-called inappropriate time, I'll be ruthless and whack a cane to the ground if necessary.

As the season chugs along, I do occasional pruning or deadheading of spent flowers on my repeat-bloomers. Often, however, I do not attend to this task religiously because it would be too time consuming considering that I grow more than one hundred roses. I am also not a fussy gardener. But if you grow only a few roses, you may choose to attend to this maintenance chore on a daily basis, snipping off the blooms when they have finished to bring on more new blossoms. How to tend to your garden tasks depends on your lifestyle, time constraints, and your degree of tidiness.

Roses and Winter Protection

I prefer not to use wood mulch in my flower beds. My mulch consists of the plants themselves, whether they are roses, perennials, shrubs, or other plant material that covers the ground. I plant thickly, which seems to eliminate the need for mulch. If your garden is smaller or you just have a few roses and perennials, wood mulch may fit your garden and your lifestyle. In November, once the ground has frozen somewhat, I'll sometimes throw a few shovelfuls of compost over the rose, particularly the newly planted ones (as I mentioned previously in the section on planting). I'll also cover certain other plants that are new to my garden in the last year or two. In truth, I just don't get around to mulching. But mulching does have benefits, including keeping the soil at an even temperature, keeping water needs down, controlling weeds, and giving an overall attractive appearance to the garden. Only a few inches of mulch are needed: more than that may invite diseases and pests to invade the garden. I recommend small wood pieces, as larger pieces take a long time to break down. Economics plays a role in mulching, too. Wood mulch is cost- and care-efficient. Some people use small rocks and gravel for a mulch. That works, too. In my gardens, I use rock mulch on my paths and in my rock gardens, although I do have about six roses in areas where I have a small amount of gravel mulch. However, aesthetically I don't like the look of a planting of only rocks and roses. Certain gardens may look satisfactory this way, but for me rocks signal dryness and I don't like the combination of rocks and roses, unless it is designed a certain way. Mulching is quicker than planting and designing a large flower bed and maintaining it, especially if you do not constantly live in your garden! Mulching is a personal and subjective choice, hotly debated in the gardening world. I encourage each gardener to discover what works for her. (For more detailed discussions on mulch, please see my book, *The Intuitive Gardener.*)

I do water newly planted roses two or three times a month during dry spells. In winter, when temperatures warm to 50 or 60 degrees, I drag out my hose and water. If this is not done—and sometimes I forget, or get too involved with inside matters—I might lose the plant, which is a terribly sad thing! These plants are like my children. They are infants and want constant love and attention when young and when they sprout new stems. Like people, they flourish with good care and bloom for the entire world to see.

Appendixes

Rose Lists

Shade-Tolerant Roses

Roses like full sun—preferably a minimum of six hours: more is ideal. There are exceptions, however—quite a few in fact. The following is a list of rose varieties that bloom well in shady settings that receive approximately three or four hours of unfiltered sunlight daily. When a rose bush receives less than three or four hours of sunlight, it will likely produce fewer blossoms and its canes will stretch toward the sunlight. Experiment with the needs of your rose: that's what a lot of gardening is all about. Remember, if your rose is not "happy," it can usually be moved to a more agreeable site.

'Alba Maxima'
'Alika' (aka *R. gallica grandiflora*)
'Baltimore Belle'
'Banshee'
'Basye's Purple Rose'
'Belle Poitevine'
'Bobbie James'
'Complicata'
'Constance Spry'
'Corylus'
'Darlow's Enigma'
'Flutterbye'
'Hansa'
'Hebe's Lip'
'Hiawatha Recurrent'
'John Cabot'
'Knock-Out'
'Lawrence Johnston'
'Linda Campbell'
'Louise Odier'
'Madame Hardy'
'Maiden's Blush'

'Marjorie Fair'
'Martin Frobisher'
'New Dawn'
'Nozomi'
'Pink Meidiland'
'Pompon Blanc Parfait'
Rosa rugosa 'Robusta'
R. eglanteria
R. rugosa alba
R. rugosa rubra
R. wichurana
R. x alba 'Semiplena'
R. foetida bicolor (Austrian copper)
R. glauca
'Rose de Rescht'
'Sparrieshoop'
'The Fairy'
'Thérèse Bugnet'
'Vanity'
'William Baffin'
'Winnipeg Parks'

Drought-Tolerant Roses

Once established, many roses can tolerate varying degrees of drought. From my experience, the following roses survive and thrive with minimal amounts of additional water—roughly three to four times a year of *deep soaking*. But much depends on Mother Nature, so exact recipes are exceedingly difficult to give. Plus there are many variables, depending on where the rose is planted. Is the site protected, or is it exposed to high winds in winter or summer that will dry out the soil? Is the rose covered with snow until the spring thaw? Is the area mulched? Does the rose receive water runoff from nearby areas? What are soil conditions like? Clay soil holds water longer than sandy soil. All these factors affect the performance of the rose and determine the amount of water your rose needs in a particular site. Look over your roses every few weeks or months. Feel the soil—and not just the top inch: put your finger or a screwdriver down a few inches into the soil to test. Is the soil moist or dry? Develop a relationship with your garden and roses—and not only in June.

'Adelaide Hoodless'
'Banshee'
'Belle Poitevine'
'Complicata'
'Harison's Yellow'
'Hiawatha Recurrent'
'John Cabot'
'Lawrence Johnston'
'Maiden's Blush'
'Martin Frobisher'
'Nearly Wild'
'Nozomi'
'Reine des Violettes'
Rosa eglanteria

R. foetida bicolor (Austrian copper)
R. foetida persiana
R. glauca
R. hugonis
R. rugosa alba
R. spinosissima
R. wichurana
'Stanwell Perpetual'
'Sydonie'
'Thérèse Bugnet'
'Variegata di Bologna'
'William Baffin'

Fragrant Roses

Often fragrance transports us to memories and connects us to people and places both past and present. We all have different and distinct tastes in terms of what scents we either like or dislike. Most of the old garden roses have a strong fragrance, but there are others that do not. This list is not the final word on scented roses—sniff your roses to smell for yourself! The scent of some roses is affected by time of day and various environmental conditions such as weather, sun, and shade. What follows are roses that have captured my attention over the years, each with a varying degree and type of fragrance, but all fragrant.

'Alba Maxima'	'Henry Hudson'
'Alchemist'	'Laneii'
'Alfred Colomb'	'Madame Hardy'
'Alika' (a.k.a. *Rosa gallica grandiflora*)	'Maiden's Blush'
'Banshee'	'Nymphenburg'
'Baronne Prévost'	'Reine des Violettes'
'Belle Poitevine'	*Rosa x. alba* 'Semiplena'
'Charles de Mills'	*R. rugosa alba*
'Darlow's Enigma'	*R. rugosa rubra*
'Désirée Parmentier'	'Rose de Rescht'
'Golden Wings'	'Sydonie'
'Harison's Yellow'	'Variegata di Bologna'
	'William Lobb'

Repeat-Blooming Roses

Roses that repeat-bloom or are continuous bloomers are highly desired by gardeners, which is why hybrid teas and floribundas are so popular. Heavy late spring and summer bloom is typical of most shrub roses. In summer and fall, there are usually fewer blossoms. From one rose variety to another, there is huge variability: some produce a few flowers, others a moderate number, and some a very slight number. Some roses rest for a few weeks in between blooming periods, at which time no flowers will appear. Intense heat can sometimes affect rose bloom. Bloom patterns vary from one variety to another and sometimes from garden to garden and year-to-year. The following roses have varying amounts of repeat-bloom after their initial spring/summer flush.

'Adelaide Hoodless'	'Morden Blush'
'Applejack'	'Morden Ruby'
'Baronne Prévost'	'Morden Snowbeauty'
'China Doll'	'Nearly Wild'
'Cuthbert Grant'	'New Face'
'Darlow's Enigma'	'Pink Meidiland'
'Dortmund'	'Robusta'
'Flower Girl'	*Rosa rugosa*
'Golden Wings'	*R. rugosa alba*
'Hansa'	*R. rugosa rubra*
'Henry Hudson'	'Rose de Rescht'
'J. P. Connell'	'Sydonie'
'Jeanne LaJoie'	'Sparrieshoop'
'Jens Munk'	'The Fairy'
'John Cabot'	'Thérèse Bugnet'
'John Davis'	'Vanity'
'Linda Campbell'	'William Baffin'
'Martin Frobisher'	

Roses with Rose Hips

Some, but not all roses produce rose hips, which are the fruits of the rose. Some roses are sterile and therefore do not produce hips. Alternatively, other roses may not produce hips because of the effects of various environmental conditions, such as water, soil, sun, and snow. Rose hips vary greatly in size, shape, and color, although most are red, roundish, and the size of a small marble. Yet others are rather tiny—smaller than the size of a pea, compared to some large, robust hips that are as much as 2 inches in length and oblong in shape. Smooth and shiny, rose hips are attractive in autumn and often remain on the shrub into winter, unless birds grab them first. The colorful hips create an excellent contrast against various shades of green leaves. In addition, they enhance the fall garden when the hips are juxtaposed with various late-blooming perennials such as asters, mums, and black-eyed Susans. As the winter chill settles in, many rose hips transform and become crinkled, which adds distinctive accents to the landscape.

'Adelaide Hoodless'
'Alba Maxima'
'Alika' (a.k.a. *Rosa gallica grandiflora*)
'Banshee'
'Belle Poitevine'
'Complicata'
'Corylus'
'Désirée Parmentier'
'Dortmund'
'Goldbusch'
'Golden Wings'
'Hansa'
'Harison's Yellow'
'Hiawatha'
'Jens Munk'
'John Cabot'
'Lawrence Johnston'
'Louise Odier'

'Morden Blush'
'New Face'
'Nozomi'
'Pink Meidiland'
Rosa eglanteria
R. glauca
R. hugonis
R. rugosa alba
R. rugosa rubra
R. spinosissima
R. wichurana
'Sparrieshoop'
'Sydonie'
'Thérèse Bugnet'
'Vanity'
'William Baffin'
'William Lobb'
'Winnipeg Parks'

Rose Companions

The beauty and fragrance of roses illuminate any garden. Their grandeur is enhanced when other flowers mingle with them to create tantalizing scenes to stroll through and admire. From ground covers to a wide assortment of annuals, to many perennials as well as shrubs, I have found the plants that follow to be excellent partners for your roses.

Annuals

Ageratum (floss flower)
borage
cosmos
dusty miller
larkspur
love-in-a-mist

red orach
spider flower
sweet alyssum
verbena—tall and short varieties
violets

Ground-cover Perennials

artemisia
catmint
coral bells
cranesbill
crosswort
lady's mantle

lamb's ears
lavender
rue
soapwort
sweet woodruff
veronica

Larger Perennials

beard tongue
bee balm
Cephalaria gigantea
checker mallow
clematis—vine
columbine
coneflower
coreopsis
delphinum
feverfew
foxglove
gas plant
gayfeather
goat's rue

Jerusalem sage
ornamental grasses—
feather reed,
miscanthus, sedge,
purple moor grass,
fountain grass,
switchgrass, tufted hair grass
ornamental onion
pinks
plume poppy
salvia
sea holly
Shasta daisy

Quick-Reference Rose Chart

This chart catalogs an assortment of roses. It is based on my experience of growing roses in my garden in Littleton, Colorado (a southwest suburb of Denver), over the past fifteen years. It also reflects my opinions and prejudices. With proper care, most of these roses will survive in temperatures of minus 25 degrees or colder. Please make any necessary adjustments to care for them in your particular garden environment. Your educated trial-and-error attempts are the best teacher. You should also seek out the wisdom and guidance of experts in your region.

Rose Name	Blossom Type	Class	Repeat-Bloom	Fragrance	Color	Climber	Hips	Height in Feet	Additional Comments
'Abraham Darby'	Double	Austin, shrub	Yes	Yes	Coppery apricot	No	No	4–5	
'Adelaide Hoodless'	Semidouble	Canadian shrub	Yes	No	Dark red	No	Some	5–7	*Extremely drought tolerant*
'Agnes'	Double	Rugosa	Some	Yes	Pale and dark yellow	No	No	3–4	
'Alain Blanchard'	Semidouble	Gallica–OGR	No	Yes	Crimson-purple	No	Some	3–4	
'Alba Maxima'	Double	Alba–OGR	No	Yes	White	Possible with good training	Yes	7–10	*Inch-long, plump, red hips*
'Alchemist'	Semidouble	Shrub	No	Yes	Apricot-gold	Yes, in warmer climates	No	5–8	*Put in a protected spot; marginally hardy*
'Alfred Colomb'	Double	Hybrid perpetual–OGR	Yes	Yes	Strawberry red	No	No	4–5	*No care, tough*
'Alika' (a.k.a. *R. gallica grandiflora*)	Semidouble	Gallica–OGR	No	Yes	Deep pink	No	Yes	5–6	*Stunning hips shaped like Hershey's Kisses; great burgundy fall color*
'America'	Double	Shrub	Yes	Yes	Orange-pink	Yes	No	8–12	
'Applejack'	Semidouble	Shrub	Yes	Yes	Pink	No	Some	5–7	*Lovely arching form*
'Ballerina'	Single	Shrub	Yes	No	Blush pink	No	Yes	3–4	
'Baltimore Belle'	Double	Shrub	No	Yes	Light pink	Yes	No	10–15	*Vigorous; semi-shade is okay. Secure up a sturdy trellis.*
'Banshee'	Semidouble	Damask–OGR	No	Yes	Pink	Yes, with some attention	Yes	5–8	*Very tough and drought tolerant*

Note: OGR—old garden rose.

Rose Name	Blossom Type	Class	Repeat-Bloom	Fragrance	Color	Climber	Hips	Height in Feet	Additional Comments
'Baronne Prévost'	Double	Hybrid perpetual– OGR	Yes	Yes	Pink	No	No	5–8	
'Basye's Purple Rose'	Single	Rugosa hybrid	Yes	Yes	Deep purple	No	No	3–4	*Unique*
'Belle de Crécy'	Double	Gallica– OGR	No	Yes	Pink and mauve	No	No	3–4	
'Belle Poitevine'	Semidouble	Rugosa hybrid	Yes	Yes	Pink	No	Yes	3–5	*Stunning when in full bloom*
'Bobbie James'	Semidouble	Shrub	No	Yes	Creamy ivory	Yes	Yes	15–30	*Vigorous; train up sturdy trellis. Succeeds in partial shade*
'Bonica'	Double	Shrub	Yes	Yes	Light pink	No	Yes	3–4	*Excellent along with 'Sea Foam' as a hedge*
'Camaieux'	Double	Gallica– OGR	No	Yes	Striped, rose purple, white	No	No	3–4	*Best of the striped*
'Cardinal de Richelieu'	Double	Gallica– OGR	No	Yes	Wine purple	No	No	4–5	*Unusual dark flower color*
'Carefree Beauty'	Semidouble	Buck, shrub	Yes	No	Pink	No	No	4–5	*Popular through-out most of the country*
'Charles de Mills'	Double	Gallica– OGR	No	Yes	Crimson-purple	No	No	5–7	
'Complicata'	Single	Gallica– OGR	No	Yes	Deep pink	No	Some	5–8	*One of the best*
'Constance Spry'	Double	Austin, shrub	No	Yes	Soft pink	No	No	5–7	
'Corylus'	Single	Rugosa hybrid	Yes	Yes	Silvery pink	No	No	4–5	*Fabulous fall color*
'Cuthbert Grant'	Semidouble	Canadian shrub	Yes	No	Velvety dark red	No	No	4–5	
'Darlow's Enigma'	Semidouble	Shrub	Yes	Yes	White	Yes	No	6–8	*Adaptable, easy to grow*
'Désireé Parmentier'	Double	Damask– OGR	No	Yes	Clear pink	No	Some	5–6	*Use in a large space, about 8 feet wide*
'Distant Drums'	Semidouble	Buck, shrub	Yes	Yes	Orchid-pink	No	No	3–4	
'Dortmund'	Single	Shrub	Yes	Some	Red	Short climber in cold regions	Yes	5–8	*Shiny green foliage; profuse amount of plump hips in fall*
'Dr. J. H. Nicholas'	Double	Shrub	Yes	Yes	Medium pink	Yes	No	6–8	*Nice leather foliage; short climber*
'Earth Song'	Double	Buck shrub	Yes	Yes	Deep pink	No	No	4–5	
'Evelyn'	Double	Austin, shrub	Yes	Yes	Apricot, yellow, pink	No	No	3–4	
'Ferdy'	Semidouble	Shrub	Some	No	Peachy pink	No	No	3–4	
'Flower Girl'	Semidouble	Shrub	Yes	Some	Soft pink	No	No	4–5	*Once established, needs minimal water*

Rose Name	Blossom Type	Class	Repeat-Bloom	Fragrance	Color	Climber	Hips	Height in Feet	Additional Comments
'Flutterbye'	Single–Semidouble	Shrub	Yes	Some	Pink, coral, white	No	No	2–3	Uncommon and eye-catching
'Frontenac'	Semidouble	Canadian shrub	Yes	No	Medium pink	No	No	3–4	
'Général Kléber'	Double	Moss–OGR	No	Yes	Medium pink	No	No	5–6	
'Goethe'	Single	Moss–OGR	No	Yes	Magenta pink	No	No	5–6	Outstanding texture and form
'Goldbusch'	Double	Shrub	Some	Yes	Peachy yellow	No	Yes	4–5	
'Golden Wings'	Single	Shrub	Yes	Yes	Yellow	No	Yes	5–7	Long, steady bloomer
'Hansa'	Semidouble	Rugosa shrub	Yes	Yes	Purple pink	No	Yes	4–6	Not too robust
'Harison's Yellow'	Semidouble	Shrub	No	Yes	Yellow	No	No	5–6	Extremely thorny
'Hawkeye Belle'	Semidouble	Buck, shrub	Yes	Some	Salmon pink	No	Yes	3–4	Slow to mature
'Hebe's Lip'	Semidouble	Damask–OGR	No	Yes	Blush white	No	No	4–5	Gorgeous skeletal form
'Henry Hudson'	Double	Canadian shrub	Yes	Yes	White	No	Some	1–2	
'Hiawatha Recurrent'	Single	Shrub	Yes	No	Crimson	Yes	Some	10–15	Great for trailing along a wall
'Hippolyte'	Double	Gallica–OGR	No	Yes	Magenta purple	No	No	3–4	
'Ispahan'	Double	Damask–OGR	No	Yes	Bright pink	No	No	4–5	
'J. P. Connell'	Semidouble	Canadian shrub	Some	Some	Pale yellow	No	No	4–6	Matures slowly
'Jeanne LaJoie'	Semidouble	Miniature	Yes	Some	Candy pink	Yes	No	5–8	
'Jens Munk'	Semidouble	Rugosa hybrid	Yes	Yes	Pink	No	Some	4–6	
'John Cabot'	Double	Canadian shrub	Yes	No	Deep pink	Yes	Yes	10–15	
'John Franklin'	Semidouble	Canadian shrub	Yes	Some	Red	No	No	3–4	
'Knock–Out'	Single	Shrub	Yes	Some	Cherry red	No	No	3–4	Performs well in minimal sun
'La Belle Sultane'	Single	Gallica–OGR	No	Yes	Crimson mauve	No	Yes	3–4	
'Laneii'	Double	Moss–OGR	No	Yes	Deep pink	No	No	3–4	
'Lawrence Johnston'	Semidouble	Shrub	Some	Some	Yellow	Yes	No	10+	Expansive; give much space
'Linda Campbell'	Semidouble	Rugosa hybrid	Yes	No	Cherry red	No	No	5–6	Almost 20 buds to a cluster
'Louise Odier'	Double	Bourbon–OGR	Yes	Yes	Pink	No	Yes	5–7	
'Madame Hardy'	Double	Damask–OGR	No	Yes	White	No	No	5–6	
'Marjorie Fair'	Single	Shrub	Yes	Some	Red/white	No	No	3–4	
'Martin Frobisher'	Semidouble	Canadian shrub	Yes	Yes	Soft pink center	No	No	5–7	Vibrant, red-tinged leaves in fall

Rose Name	Blossom Type	Class	Repeat-Bloom	Fragrance	Color	Climber	Hips	Height in Feet	Additional Comments
'Mary Rose'	Double	Austin, shrub	Yes	Some	Rose pink	No	Yes	4–5	
'May Queen'	Semidouble	Shrub	No	Some	Rose pink	Yes	No	5–8	Low climber, thin stems
'Metis'	Semidouble	Shrub	No	Some	Pink	No	No	3–4	Thin, wiry stems
'Morden Blush'	Double	Canadian shrub	Yes	No	Blush pink	No	Yes	3–4	Longest-blooming Canadian
'Morden Ruby'	Semidouble	Canadian shrub	Yes	No	Deep pink	No	No	4–5	Some petal edges silvery white
'Morden Snowbeauty'	Single	Canadian shrub	Yes	Some	White	No	No	1–2	Striking single blooms
'Morden Sunrise'	Single	Canadian shrub	Yes	No	yellow, orange, pink, white	No	No	2–3	multi-colored
'Nearly Wild'	Single	Shrub	Yes	Some	Pink/white	No	No	3–4	Easy and very reliable
'Nevada'	Single	Shrub	Some	Yes	White	No	No	5–7	Chocolate thornless stems
'New Dawn'	Double	Shrub	Yes	Yes	Silvery blush pink	Yes	Some	10–15	Fast grower
'New Face'	Single	Shrub	Yes	No	Pink, white, yellow	No	Some	5–7	
'Nozomi'	Single	Shrub	No	No	Pinky white	Yes, taller in warmer climates	Some	4–6	
'Nymphenburg'	Semidouble	Shrub	Some	Yes	Apricot-pink	No	Some	5–7	
'Pink Meidiland'	Single	Shrub	Yes	No	Pink and white	No	Yes	3–4	
'Pompon Blanc Parfait'	Double	Alba–OGR	No	Yes	Pale lilac	No	No	4–6	Nearly thornless stems; slow to mature
'Prairie Flower'	Single	Buck, shrub	Yes	Some	Cardinal red	No	No	4–5	
'Queen Nefertiti'	Double	Shrub	Yes	Yes	Yellowish, apricot pink	No	No	3–4	Marginally hardy in cold climates; remember to mulch
'Raubritter'	Double	Shrub	No	No	Cherry pink	No	No	3–4	Robust, big blooms
'Reine des Violettes'	Double	Hybrid perpetual–OGR	Yes	Yes	Violet	No	No	5–7	
'Robusta'	Single	Shrub	Yes	Yes	Crimson red	No	No	4–5	Exceptional fall color
Rosa alba 'Maiden's Blush'	Double	Alba–OGR	No	Yes	Blush white	No	Yes	5–6	Suckers a great deal
Rosa x alba 'Semiplena'	Double	Alba–OGR	No	Yes	White	No	Yes	5–8	Shiny, big red hips
Rosa arkansana	Single	Species	No	Yes	Clear pink	No	Yes	1–2	
Rosa blanda	Single	Species	No	No	Pale pink	No	Yes	3–4	Almost thornless, mildly suckering stems
Rosa canina	Single	Species	No	Yes	Pale pink	Can be trained	Yes	6–8	Vigorous and large

Rose Name	Blossom Type	Class	Repeat-Bloom	Fragrance	Color	Climber	Hips	Height in Feet	Additional Comments
Rosa eglanteria	Single	Species	No	Yes	Clear pink	Yes	Yes	10–15	Foliage smells like apple
Rosa filipes 'Kiftsgate'	Single	Shrub	No	Yes	Creamy white	No	Yes	n/a	Vigorous, but not hardy in cold climates
Rosa foetida bicolor syn. 'Austrian Copper'	Single	Species	No	Yes	Orange-red	No	No	5–7	A bit scraggly looking
Rosa foetida persiana	Double	Species	No	Yes	Yellow	No	No	5–7	Keep suckers cut down
Rosa glauca or rubrifolia	Single	Species	No	No	Pink and white	No	Yes	5–7	Exceptional fall color
Rosa hugonis	Single	Species	Yes	Yes	Bright yellow	No	Some	5–7	Fast-growing; thin out old stems often
Rosa moyesii 'Geranium'	Single	Shrub	No	Some	Bright red	No	Yes	5–8	
Rosa multiflora	Single	Species	No	Yes	White	No	No	5–8	Large, aggressive, not very thorny canes
'Rosa Mundi' (a.k.a. R. gallica versicolor)	Double	Gallica–OGR	No	Yes	Striped crimson and white	No	Yes	3–4	
Rosa pulverulenta	Single	Species	No	No	Clear pink	No	Some forms	3–5	Pine-scented foliage
Rosa rugosa alba	Single	Species	Yes	Yes	White	No	Yes	3–5	
Rosa rugosa rubra	Single	Species	Yes	Yes	Raspberry-pink	No	Yes	3–5	
Rosa sericea pteracantha	Single	Species	No	No	White	Yes	Yes	n/a	Not hardy in cold climates; needs temperatures approx. 40 degrees or warmer
Rosa spinosissima	Single	Species	No	Some	White	No	Some	4–5	Every two or three years, cut out suckers
Rosa spinosissima altaica	Single	Species	No	Some	Soft yellow	No	Yes	4–5	Cherry-size black hips; unusual
Rosa wichurana	Single	Species	No	Yes	White	Yes	No	10–15	Thornless; roots easily; great ground cover
Rosa xanthina	Single	Species	No	Some	Light yellow	No	Yes	5–6	
'Rose de Meaux'	Double	Centifolia–OGR	No	Yes	Shell pink	No	No	3	A bit fussy
'Rose de Rescht'	Double	Portland–OGR	Yes	Yes	Magenta	No	No	3–4	Tight, compact form
'Salet'	Quartered	Moss–OGR	Some	Yes	Pink	No	Yes	2–3	Few thorns
'Sea Foam'	Semidouble	Shrub	Yes	No	White	No	No	3–4	Easy and robust
'Sir Thomas Lipton'	Double	Rugosa hybrid	Yes	Yes	White	No	No	5–7	
'Sissinghurst Castle'	Semidouble	Gallica–OGR	No	Yes	Red	No	No	3–4	Few thorns
'Sparrieshoop'	Single	Shrub	Yes	Yes	Rosy pink	No	Some	4–5	
'Stanwell Perpetual'	Double	Shrub	No	Yes	Light pink	No	No	3–4	Tough and reliable

Rose Name	Blossom Type	Class	Repeat-Bloom	Fragrance	Color	Climber	Hips	Height in Feet	Additional Comments
'Starry Night'	Single	Shrub	Yes	No	White	No	No	2–3	Bushy form; profuse, long bloomer
'Sydonie'	Double	Damask–OGR	Yes	Yes	Pink	No	No	4–5	
'Thérèse Bugnet	Double	Rugosa hybrid	Yes	Yes	Lilac-pink	No	No	5–7	Rich fall color
'Tuscany'	Semidouble	Gallica–OGR	No	Yes	White-flecked maroon	No	No	3–4	
'Tuscany Superb'	Semidouble	Gallica–OGR	No	Yes	Maroon	No	No	3–4	
'Vanity'	Single	Shrub	Yes	Yes	Deep pink	No	Some	5–6	Lanky—plant between shrubs. Blooms late into November; worth any effort
'Variegata di Bologna'	Double	Shrub	Some	Yes	Striped	No	No	5–7	Highly prone to mildew
'Village Maid'	Double	Centifolia–OGR	Some	Yes	Off-white, streaked pink	No	No	3–4	
'Wild Ginger'	Semidouble	Buck, shrub	Yes	Yes	Apricot-orange	No	No	4–5	
'William Baffin'	Semidouble	Canadian shrub	Yes	No	Raspberry	Yes	Some	10–15	Expansive, give much space
'William Booth'	Single	Canadian shrub	Yes	No	Deep red	Yes	Yes	7–10	
'William Lobb'	Semidouble	Moss–OGR	No	Yes	Crimson-purple	No	Yes	5–8	
'Winnipeg Parks'	Semidouble	Canadian shrub	Yes	Some	Red	No	Yes	3–4	Outstanding burgundy foliage in fall and on new growth

Select Mail-Order Rose Catalogs

Most of the rose sources listed below have nurseries you can visit, should you live nearby. All ship their roses throughout North America. Study the information on their Web sites to learn if a particular rose is suitable for your growing zone. Or call them directly to get growing advice. Most have toll-free numbers.

United States

Midwest

Sam Kedem Nursery
12414 191st St. E.
Hastings MN 55033
Phone: (651) 437-7516
Web site: www.kedemroses.com

Northeast

Lowe's Roses
6 Sheffield Rd.
Nashua, NH 03062
Phone: (603) 888-2214
Web site: http://loweroses.com
Unusual species and old garden roses. Own-root. Good selection. Must order eighteen months ahead.

Southeast

Ashdown Roses
P.O.B. 129
Campobello, SC 29322-0129
Phone: 1 864-468-4900
E-mail: roses@ashdownroses.com
Web site: www.ashdownroses.com

Roses Unlimited
363 N. Deerwood Dr.
Laurens, SC 29360
Phone: (864) 682-7673
Web site:
www.rosesunlimitedownroot.com

Southwest

The Antique Rose Emporium
9300 Lueckmeyer Rd.
Brenham, TX 77833-6453
Phone: (800) 441-0002
Web site:
www.antiqueroseemporium.com
Large selection, good reference guide.

High Country Roses
P. O. Box 148
Jensen, UT 84035
Phone: (800) 552-2082
Web site: www.highcountryroses.com
Great selection, own-root in quart-sized pots. I've been pleased with what they have sent me.

West

Arena Rose Co.
Retail store: 1041 Paso Robles St.
Paso Robles, CA 93446
Phone: (888) 466-7434
Web site: www.arenaroses.com
In 2006, this company offered nearly 400 varieties of bare-root roses.

Forestfarm
990 Tetherow Rd.
Williams, OR 97544-9599
Phone: (541) 846-7269
Web site: www.forestfarm.com
Good selection of species and shrub roses on their own roots. I've ordered from them for years and have been very pleased.

Heirloom Old Garden Roses
24062 N.E. Riverside Dr.
St. Paul, OR 97137
Phone: (800) 820-0465
Web site: www.heirloomroses.com
Good selection of old garden roses, shrub roses, David Austins, and more. Own-root. I've been very satisfied with selections I have ordered.

Vintage Gardens
2833 Old Gravenstein Hwy. S.
Sebastopol, CA 95472
Phone: (707) 829-2035
Web site: www.vintagegardens.com
Large selection, excellent and thorough descriptions.

Canada

Corn Hill Nursery, Ltd.
2700 Route 890
Corn Hill, New Brunswick E4Z 1M2
Canada
Phone: (506) 756-3635
Web site: www.cornhillnursery.com
Specialist in hardy roses, most own-root, shipping bare-root April 15–May 15.

Hortico
723 Robson Rd., RR #1
Waterdown, Ontario L0R 2H1
Canada
Phone: (905) 689-6984
Web site: www.hortico.com
Very large selection. Good descriptions.

Pickering Nurseries, Inc.
3043 County Rd. #2, RR #1
Port Hope, Ontario L1A 3V5
Canada
Phone: (866) 269-9282
Web site: www.pickeringnurseries.com

Rose Societies and Organizations

American Rose Society

www.ars.org
1-800-637-6534
Magazine

Heritage Roses Group

Mostly focuses on Old Garden roses, species, and the unusual
Newsletter
www.heritagerosesgroup.org

The Royal National Rose Society

www.rnrs.org

American Rose Rambler

Provides the latest up-to-date information on all aspects of roses
Peter Schneider
P.O.B. 677
Mantua OH 44255
330-296-2618
email: Peter@combinedroselist.com
Newsletter

The Combined Rose List

This softcover book, published annually, is a comprehensive listing of
    essential information on all roses in commerce, both in the U.S.
    and abroad
www.combinedroselist.com
303-296-2618
email: ComRoseLst@cs.com

Bibliography

Agriculture and Agri-Food Canada. *Winter Hardy Roses.* Publication 1922/E. Ottawa: Minister of Public Works and Government Services, Canada, 1996.

Armitage, Allan M. *Armitage's Garden Perennials: A Color Encyclopedia.* Portland, OR: Timber Press, 2000.

Austin, David. *David Austin's English Roses: Glorious New Roses for American Gardens.* New York: Little, Brown and Co., 1997.

Barnette, Martha. *A Garden of Words.* New York: Random House, Inc., 1992.

Bath, Trevor, and Joy Jones. *The Gardener's Guide to Growing Hardy Geraniums.* Portland, OR: Timber Press, 1994.

Beales, Peter. *Roses.* New York: Henry Holt and Co., 1992.

Clausen, Ruth Rogers, and Nicolas H. Ekstrom. *Perennials for American Gardens.* New York: Random House, 1989.

Darke, Rick. *The Color Encyclopedia of Ornamental Grasses: Sedges, Rushes, Restios, Cat-tails, and Selected Bamboos.* Portland, OR: Timber Press, 1999.

Dickerson, Brent C. *The Old Rose Adventurer: The Once-Blooming Old European Roses, and More.* Portland, OR: Timber Press, 1999.

———. *The Old Rose Advisor.* Portland, OR: Timber Press, 1992.

Druitt, Liz. *The Organic Rose Garden.* Dallas, TX: Taylor Publishing Company, 1996.

Fretwell, Barry. *Clematis as Companion Plants.* New York: Sterling Publishing Co., Inc. 1995.

Graham, Marlea. "The Hundred Years' War: Own-root vs. Budded Roses." *American Rose Annual* vol. XXI, no. 24 (1994).

Greenlee, John. *The Encyclopedia of Ornamental Grasses: How to Grow and Use Over 250 Beautiful and Versatile Plants.* Emmaus, PA: Rodale Press, 1992.

Grey-Wilson, Christopher. *Poppies: The Poppy Family in the Wild and in Cultivation.* Portland, OR: Timber Press, 1993.

Hansen, Richard, and Friedrich Stahl. *Perennials and Their Garden Habitats.* Portland, OR: Timber Press, 1993.

Irwin, Pamela D. *Colorado's Best Wildflower Hikes. Vol. 2: The High Country.* Eglewood, CO: Westcliffe Publishing, Inc., 1999.

Joyce, David (Christopher Brickell, technical consultant). *Pruning and Training Plants: The Complete Guide.* Buffalo, NY: FireFly Books, 2001.

Kowalchik, Claire, and William Hylton, eds. *Rodale's Illustrated Encyclopedia of Herbs.* Emmaus, PA: Rodale Press, 1987.

Lacy, Allen. *The Glory of Roses.* New York: Stewart, Tabori and Chang, 1990.

Loewer, Peter. *The Annual Garden.* Emmaus, PA: Rodale Press, 1995.

McKeon, Judith C. *Gardening with Roses: Designing with Easy-Care Climbers, Ramblers, and Shrubs.* New York: Friedman/Fairfax Publishing, 1997.

Olds, Margaret, ed. *Botanicas Roses.* New York: Random House, Mynah, 1998.

Osborne, Robert. *Hardy Roses: An Organic Guide to Growing Frost- and Disease-Resistant Varieties.* Pownal, VT: Storey Communications, Inc., 1991.

Ottesen, Carole. *Ornamental Grasses: The Amber Wave.* San Francisco: McGraw-Hill Publishing Co., Inc. 1989.

Phillips, Roger, and Martyn Rix. *The Quest for the Rose: A Historical Guide to Roses.* New York: Random House, 1994.

Raff, Marilyn. *The Intuitive Gardner: Finding Creative Freedom in the Garden.* Golden, CO: Fulcrum Publishing, 2002.

Reilly, Ann. *The Rose.* New York: Portland House, 1989.

Schoup, Michael G., and Liz Druitt. *Landscaping with Antique Roses.* Newton, CT: The Taunton Press, 1992.

Springer, Lauren. *The Undaunted Garden: Planting for Weather-Resilient Beauty.* Golden, CO: Fulcrum Publishing, 1994.

Thomas, Graham Stuart. *Perennial Garden Plants: Or the Modern Florilegium: A Concise Account of Herbaceous Plants, Including Bulbs, for General Garden Use.* Portland, OR: Timber Press, 1990.

———. *Ornamental Shrubs, Climbers and Bamboo: Excluding Roses and Rhododendrons.* Portland, OR: Timber Press, 1992.

———. *The Graham Stuart Thomas Rose Book.* Portland, OR: Timber Press, 1994.

Turner, Roger. *Euphorbias: A Gardener's Guide.* Portland, OR: Timber Press, 1995.

Verrier, Suzanne. *Rosa Gallica.* Deer Park, WI: Capability's Books, 1995.

———. *Rosa Rugosa.* Deer Park, WI: Capability's Books, 1991.

Wells, Diane. *100 Flowers and How They Got Their Names.* Chapel Hill, NC: Algonquin Books of Chapel Hill, 1997.

Zuzek, Kathy, Marcia Richards, Steve McNamara, and Harold Pellett. "Roses for the North." *Minnesota Report* 237-1995. St. Paul, MN: Minnesota Agricultural Experiment Station, University of Minnesota.

Index